It's Only Temporary

It's Only Temporary

THE GOOD NEWS AND

THE BAD NEWS OF BEING ALIVE

Evan Handler

RIVERHEAD BOOKS

a member of Penguin Group (USA) Inc.

New York

2008

RIVERHEAD BOOKS
Published by the Penguin Group
Penguin Group (USA) Inc., 375 Hudson Street, New York, New York 10014, USA · Penguin Group
(Canada), 90 Eglinton Avenue East, Suite 700, Toronto, Ontario M4P 2Y3, Canada (a division of
Pearson Canada Inc.) · Penguin Books Ltd, 80 Strand, London WC2R 0RL, England · Penguin
Ireland, 25 St Stephen's Green, Dublin 2, Ireland (a division of Penguin Books Ltd) · Penguin Group
(Australia), 250 Camberwell Road, Camberwell, Victoria 3124, Australia (a division of Pearson
Australia Group Pty Ltd) · Penguin Books India Pvt Ltd, 11 Community Centre, Panchsheel Park,
New Delhi–110 017, India · Penguin Group (NZ), 67 Apollo Drive, Rosedale, North Shore 0632,
New Zealand (a division of Pearson New Zealand Ltd) · Penguin Books (South Africa) (Pty) Ltd,
24 Sturdee Avenue, Rosebank, Johannesburg 2196, South Africa

Penguin Books Ltd, Registered Offices: 80 Strand, London WC2R 0RL, England

Library of Congress Cataloging-in-Publication Data

Handler, Evan.
It's only temporary : the good news and the bad news of being alive / Evan Handler.
p.   cm.
ISBN 978-1-59448-995-2
1. Handler, Evan—Health.   2. Acute myeloid leukemia—Patients—United States—Biography.
I. Title.
RC643.H285   2008   2008005404
362.196'994190092—dc22
[B]

Printed in the United States of America
1   3   5   7   9   10   8   6   4   2

Book design by Chris Welch

While the author has made every effort to provide accurate telephone numbers and Internet addresses
at the time of publication, neither the publisher nor the author assumes any responsibility for errors,
or for changes that occur after publication. Further, the publisher does not have any control over and
does not assume any responsibility for author or third-party websites or their content.

Throughout this book, the names of some places as well as individuals and their personal details have
been changed.

Per Elisa . . .

Tu ed io, insieme, per sempre

Contents

If pleasure exists, and we can only enjoy it in life,
then life is happiness.

—Giacomo Casanova, 1725-1798

Call no man happy until he is dead.

—Solon of Athens, c. 638-558 b.c.

Preface

I've never been a fan of explaining myself before I've begun, or of those who make it a practice. Then again, Oscar Wilde wrote introductions to many of his works, and some of them said what the book said much better than the book did, and in one one-hundred-twenty-fifth the space. Then again—again—Oscar Wilde went to prison and died at forty-six. He wasn't greatly appreciated in his day.

David Mamet, another writer I admire, often inserts poems or song lyrics at the beginning of his books and plays. He credits each snippet, upon publication, as being an "ancient folktune," or some such, only to reveal later that he simply made it up. But David Mamet is far cleverer than I'll ever be, and I've got to live with that every day.

Which brings us to this book, and why it hasn't (officially) started yet. As I've been published or quoted over the years, I've noticed that each utterance I make offers infinite opportunities for misunderstanding. No matter how clearly I think I've put my message across, I'll be surprised to learn I've failed to convey what it is I meant, or to anticipate the prisms of each and every reader's mind. So I'll say it as best I can: this is a book about perspective, and how it can change. It's a book about how there are times when it's great to be alive, and other times when you might wish you'd never been born (speaking thematically, that is; in literal terms it's about growing up late in the game, transcending a depression, and learning to live with something some might describe as post-traumatic stress disorder—but that much, at least, should be clear). It's a book about how one man finally learned to live well in the world, in spite of possessing the knowledge that his life—like everyone's—will be of limited duration.

These might seem like rudimentary principles for a forty-five-year-old to be coming to terms with. But, if you're anything like me, you've learned that what seems like one thing today can come to have completely different meaning tomorrow (or two weeks, or two years, from now). If you're anything like me, you've probably learned that same thing over and over—then had more learning to do. My first book, *Time on Fire*, was about how events caused me to be disappointed by my own life story. This book is about how further events have allowed me to fall in love with it.

THIS IS ALSO A BOOK I've attempted to write in a manner that mimics how we get to know other human beings more accurately than a traditional narrative. In my experience, information doesn't flow from new acquaintances in chronological order. What I most often get is a growing compilation of stories and reflections, told out of order, many of which overlap, and refer again and again to a set of shared events and characters. Questions about these new associates often come to mind weeks, months, or even years before they're answered. Details about their significant others might not be shared with me until well after that particular relationship is over, and the subject of discussion long gone. Often, new details about my new friends dramatically alter the first impressions that had already begun to form. Only over time, as the stories add up and blank spots on the canvas are filled in, do I feel I've come to "know" someone.

Which is all to say that, should you find portions of this book—like a new friend—confusing, I urge you to keep reading. The information you crave is likely around the corner, in the next story—or the one after that. For that matter, should you initially find aspects of your new acquaintance's personality to be trying, like everything in life, that personality is bound to change. In fact, it's part of the point. A transformation lies ahead. Just as there can be no "middles" or "endings" without "beginnings," there can't be an "after" without its "before." And we often can't begin to know where it is we've been until we've traveled somewhere else and are able to look back.

—E.H.

It's Only Temporary

"Separation" Anxiety

I'M IN THE MINUSCULE, windowless bathroom of my apartment in Manhattan's East Village. I'm standing over the sink, in the most cramped region of a poorly designed space, holding a scrap of fabric embedded with human hair. My own head is only partially covered with clumps of billowy wisps resembling what you'd find on newborn babies, or people with eight toes in the grave. I'm twenty-eight years old. I'm preparing to put on a wig.

I attach a large piece of double-sided tape to the wig's fragile fabric, known as "netting," at each side of the wig's neckline in back. This is done by carefully peeling off just one side of the tape's paper backing, then pressing the exposed sticky side into the wig's interior. The netting of the wig is really hardly "fabric" at all. It's a loose weave of delicate threads nearly as slim as the tens of thousands of hairs that have been hand-tied onto them to give the impression of a full head of hair.

Once the piece of tape is attached, I fold back one corner to aid in peeling off the other paper side once the whole contraption is on my head. It's a tricky procedure, as the tape will often stick to my fingers more securely than it will to the wig's netting. And, of course, that netting is nearly as delicate as tissue paper. I've got to be careful not to tear it. Once this step has been accomplished, I attach smaller pieces of tape inside each temple and the base of each sideburn. I bend forward to fit the helmet of hair over my skull. When I lift my head and see myself in the mirror, it's like I'm looking back in time.

Not very far back. My hair expired in April of 1988. I'm in the bathroom in January of 1990. I'm trying to grow accustomed to a routine that I wish wasn't.

My hair follicles suffered permanent damage as a result of medical treatments I'd completed eighteen months earlier. I bought the wig to pursue acting jobs, the work I did before my career—and everything else in my life—was swept aside by a diagnosis of acute myeloid leukemia. The wig makes me look exactly the way I looked before I disappeared from view some years earlier. It is used to disguise myself into appearing unchanged.

Wearing the wig is uncomfortable, both physically and psychologically. Perhaps this has something to do with the odd looks I get from neighbors when they see me in the elevator, suddenly transformed from completely bald—other than the odd fluff that grew in over the first year—to sporting a full head of hair in the hour since they last saw me. That response has been less discomfiting than the friends who don't recognize me, and whom I've had to reintroduce myself to, whenever I wear the wig out in public. A Pakistani shopkeeper in the neighborhood looked as if he was going to faint during my second trip to his store one day. The first time I had hair, the second I didn't.

"Do you have a brother?" he demanded, over and over. "Do you have a brother? There is someone else . . . someone just like you!"

Just like me indeed.

. . .

I'M PUTTING ON the wig for an important audition. Not only is it for an exceptional play at a top-tier off-Broadway theater, but the casting director working on the project is a man who has refused to see me since I offended him several years ago. We were at a party, surrounded by mutual friends from the New York theater community. The casting director was gracious enough to offer me a compliment.

"You're a good actor, Evan," he said.

"The best," was my response.

Everyone who heard the comment was taken aback. Some conversations stopped.

"There are a lot of good actors," he countered.

"Yes," I agreed. "But I'm the best. I'm the best actor in New York."

It was an appalling statement, especially in light of the company we were in. The room was filled with friends and coworkers of all the actors I'd just backhandedly disparaged. It was an idiotic and immature thing to say—a desperate attempt to elevate the compliment as high as I wished it would have gone. Still, it's not as if I threw over a table. I didn't slap anyone.

For years afterward, the man at the party didn't call me in to audition for a single role in any of his projects. When I heard about a new play everyone was excited about from other actors who'd been in for appointments already, I decided some old-fashioned groveling was in order. I called up the casting director and asked if I could come in to talk. I hoped that an apology, coupled with my near-death from leukemia and the four years I'd lost fighting to overcome it, might be enough to wipe the slate clean.

I put on the wig for our meeting. The casting director hadn't seen me since I vanished from the scene years earlier, and probably had no idea how drastically my appearance had been altered. That was another reason for my seeing him. I wanted to show myself off as relatively unchanged before he ran into me on the street and formed opinions of his own.

I walked through the cold underground corridors of the theater where the casting director worked, my scalp slick with sweat. The tape holding the wig had already worked its way loose on one side in back. I kept pressing my fingers into my temple, hoping that the tape there wouldn't give way and reveal me as the impostor I was. On a mission of reparations, impersonating the young man I used to be.

Over the preceding five years, my existence had been all but erased. I had been everything but obliterated. In January of 1990, the fact of my existence was the only thing I possessed. And I was lucky just to have that.

Not that I was feeling fortunate. I knew the statistics, and how unlikely it was for me to be alive at all. But having barely survived acute leukemia; having lost the majority of the previous five years to its treatment and the treatment's aftermath; having lost my status as a "promising newcomer" in the theater and film worlds (hell, having lost my ability to ever qualify for "newcomer" status again); having exhausted the girlfriend who'd seen me through the illness, but who'd finally left me to be with someone else ("He laughs at comic books," was the final reason she gave, while I'd lost my ability to laugh at all); having lost my hair and all vestiges of the youthful exuberance it symbolized; having lost, in a sense, my very *place in line*, "lucky" is not what I was feeling. Don't get me wrong, I knew I *was*. But I sure wasn't feeling it.

THE CASTING DIRECTOR and I had a pleasant chat. We discussed agents, and he gave me advice for reinvigorating my career. I made sure to tell him that, despite the overwhelming odds against it and the supposedly "incurable" nature of the illness I'd encountered, I was now officially categorized as permanently cured of leukemia.

I'd had several courses of the most intensive chemotherapy known to man at Memorial Sloan-Kettering Cancer Center in New York. It was a hospital I'd found to be saturated by arrogance and rife with practices that made the chances for recovery even more remote than might ordinarily be expected from an incurable illness. There was a drastic nursing shortage when I was a patient at Sloan-Kettering and the staff seemed overburdened and underinspired. Over the course of my hospitalizations there I'd been medicated with intravenous drugs labeled with the names of patients other than myself, pressured to accept ill-advised and invasive procedures, and handled by staff members who refused to follow the hospital's posted hygiene precautions for touching immunosuppressed patients like myself. Worse, whenever I complained about any of those transgressions or tried to improve the quality of the care I was getting, I was scolded and derided as being ungrateful. "Why can't you be more like Andy down the hall?" a nurse once asked after administering my crucially timed antibiotic three hours after its prescribed hour. "He comes around and helps us make the beds."

The facilities were in worse condition than the staff. The wheels of IV poles were stuck or broken off, rendering patients immobile for the duration of their stays, which could last weeks or months. I went on daily pillaging expeditions to other floors because there weren't enough sheets and pillowcases to go around.

The illness and the institution weren't the only treacherous aspects of the ordeal. The chemotherapy regimens I endured were extremely dangerous. By the time I'd passed through a first remission, had a recurrence, and achieved a second remission, half of those who'd been diagnosed and treated over a similar two-year time frame were already dead.

The problem with second remissions was that they were known to last, on average, only half as long as a first remission. Another recurrence was expected, it would most likely occur quickly, and third remissions were essentially unheard-of. I traveled two hundred miles south to Johns Hopkins Hospital in Baltimore, where I was admitted to the bone marrow transplant unit. That procedure would offer what I'd been told was the only hope left for survival. It also offered the possibility of a host of complications that added up to a twenty-five percent risk of death from the transplant procedure itself. Of those who survived the transplant, a full fifty percent would soon relapse and die of leukemia anyway.

I DIDN'T SHARE those details of my past with the casting director. I'd already learned that the majority of the information pertaining to my recent existence was too much for most people to handle. I don't blame anyone for that. I wouldn't want to be cornered by anyone who'd been through what I'd been through, either.

But I did make sure to bring to the casting director's attention a graph that had been published in *The New England Journal of Medicine*. It showed that the overwhelming majority of recurrences of acute myeloid leukemia after bone marrow transplantation occurred within twelve months. After that, the expectation was that the leukemia would not return. I wanted to make sure he understood, and that the world would soon know, that I was four months shy of two years. I would have liked to have a whole lot more meadow behind me, but I was officially out of the woods.

The casting director listened, and responded with appropriate expressions of sympathy over what I'd been forced to endure. He asked, as people sometimes do, just how lucky I'd needed to be to make it all the way through. "What percentage end up okay?" he asked.

"Beginning to end? I think about one in ten."

Letting loose with that kind of information tends to put a crimp in any conversation, so I used the lull to offer my apology. I told him I was aware that I'd handled my past professional frustrations badly. I attributed my tactlessness to youth, and to the misguided notion that the way to be considered superior was to behave as if I were. I'd been more than humbled, I said, and I hoped that whatever had transpired in the past wouldn't interfere with our being able to work together in the future.

"Oh, Evan. That's all water under the bridge," he told me. "That was all a long time ago. I'm just glad to hear you're feeling better and are ready to work."

Excellent, I thought. This is going very well.

Then he added, "Of course, I think a person's emotional health has a lot to do with their physical health, so I wasn't surprised to hear you'd gotten sick."

I FELT MY face flush, then did my best to push the color back down below my neck. I took a few breaths, but chose not to get angry. Or, more accurately, I chose not to show how angry I was. I didn't ask the questions that formed in my mind: "So, I got what I deserved? Is that what you're saying? Acute leukemia in exchange for acting like an asshole?" I did some quick estimations, figuring that if arrogance and insensitivity were all it took to cause cancer, people would be getting diagnosed by the tens of millions every day. I didn't throw over a table, though, and I didn't slap anyone this time, either. I didn't even say anything stupid. In fact, I didn't say anything at all. I just nodded. I accepted the blow, and waited for what I hoped would come next.

"Here," the casting director said as he reached toward a stack of scripts behind him. "We're casting a new play by John Guare. You should take a look at the role of Doug."

And so I got the chance to audition for Lincoln Center Theater's world premiere production of *Six Degrees of Separation*.

JOHN GUARE'S PLAY, to be directed by Jerry Zaks, was already the most coveted gig in town, months before rehearsals were scheduled to start. The gossip circulating around was that the role of Doug was already all but locked up by a young actor I'd often competed against for parts. He'd already had a big success a few years earlier at Lincoln Center with another Guare play, *The House of Blue Leaves*, which had also been directed by Zaks. Some of the same competitiveness that landed me in hot water in the first place started to reemerge. If I could snatch this role away, I thought, I'll have not only won a battle, I'll have won the war. That other actor will be vanquished. And get the role I did.

The other actor's name was Ben Stiller. Now you know the level of my skill in military analysis.

I wore the wig to the first day of rehearsals. Since I'd gotten the role based on a certain appearance—a certain deception, if you will—I felt it was my responsibility to show up for work looking the same way I'd looked when I'd convinced them to hire me. As far as I knew, no one at the theater was aware that it wasn't my hair they were seeing on my head. If I'd shown up for the first day of work without the wig, it would have looked as if a different actor had walked into the room.

But I didn't want to be stuck with putting the damn thing on every day, and I didn't want to spend my whole life pretending and hiding behind it. It made me self-conscious, not to mention more than a little concerned about the possibility of it getting accidentally knocked askew, or falling off. Even if all eventual revelations of my wig-wearing status were intentional, that lifestyle had the potential for some mighty awkward second and third dates. Sexually active singles are generally used to taking off their clothes in front of each other. I'm not sure how many women have seen their date remove the hair from his head.

At the end of the first day's rehearsal I approached Jerry Zaks. My assumption was that everyone in the theater community knew the general facts of my health history. People like to talk, and a prominent twenty-four-year-old diagnosed with a dreaded illness is fairly big news. But that didn't mean they knew my still-hirsute appearance had been so handcrafted. Jerry only knew me from my auditions and whatever reputation I might have had, so I tried to explain the situation.

"Ummm . . . actually . . . you see . . . this is a wig on my head."

Jerry's face registered no ability to comprehend what he was being told. Either that, or he was trying so hard not to let his eyes wander up to my hairline he *looked* as if he couldn't comprehend. The role I was playing was that of a healthy, mainstream college student. I asked Jerry if it would be all right if I left the hair at home for the next few weeks, until we got into dress rehearsals and costumes. I suggested we could then add back the wig, which I'd wear to make sure my appearance was appropriate for the play's performances.

"Yes, yes, of course," Jerry stammered. "Whatever makes you comfortable."

I was relieved. But "comfortable" was more than I could have hoped for.

SIX DEGREES OF SEPARATION was an enormous hit, not only over the course of its original off-Broadway run in Lincoln Center's Mitzi Newhouse Theater, but also for the length of its Broadway run in the larger Vivian Beaumont. The show, or at least its title, etched itself into the vernacular of the nation. Theatrical productions like that are rarities, and being involved in creating one is about the most exciting thing a show business career can offer. From our first invited-audience dress rehearsal, when the crowd exploded with laughter and appreciation, it became clear we were in for a spectacular ride.

But the *Six Degrees* . . . experience was made even more special by a confluence of events just as difficult to cultivate as creative magic. The cast of *Six Degrees* . . . coalesced into a collection of friendships of rare depth and intensity. Several of my closest friends nearly twenty years later are actors I met during the run of that show.

We played to sold-out crowds and overwhelming critical response. We traveled Manhattan as members of an envied clan. The roles in the play were split along generational lines: there was a group of parents and their friends, and there were their teenage and just-beyond-teenage offspring. Almost all of us playing the younger set were in our mid- to late twenties. We were almost all single. We were dating. We were almost all involved in psychotherapy of one sort or another. We were, essentially, searching for our adulthoods while being paid to portray children. But while the other young members of the cast were rushing enthusiastically into the future, I was trying to keep up, haunted by my preview of where we were all eventually headed.

What did I have in common with those other twenty-five-year-olds? We were engaged in similar activities, but our frames of reference were worlds apart. I remember hours spent backstage, over months and months, laughing at one another's dating debacles from recent years. Inverted nipples, lost erections, the wrong bodily fluids making unwanted escapes; nothing was too private or grotesque to mention. I generally tried to monitor which stories I shared with my cast mates. One night I dove in without thinking.

I recounted an anomaly I encountered in the hospital not long before. The more debilitated I got from my medical treatments, the more turned on I got. I'd never been hornier than when my life was ebbing away, I said. I figured it had something to do with the body sensing its extinction and wanting to propagate. I told them how my ex-girlfriend and I had had sex in the hospital bathroom while a comatose roommate, rendered senseless by a suspected brain tumor the doctors hadn't been able to locate, lay in bed on the other side of the door, only inches away. My girlfriend didn't even need to be there. I held my thumb and forefinger a quarter inch apart.

"I jerked off this close to death," I said, smiling.

I looked up to see a roomful of stricken faces. Hands covered mouths in horror. One of the women started to cry. I thought I'd said something funny. Instead I'd ruined everyone's good time.

It didn't seem fair. Weren't we telling our horror stories? I'd thought that was the game. It was as if I'd shown up at a Halloween party where everyone was dressed as skeletons, only I'd brought along a real cadaver.

I FELT CUT OFF. Isolated. Friendships are generally based on shared experience. I didn't know anyone my age who could identify with where I'd been, or even anyone twenty or thirty years older. The only companion I had during the dark days was my ex-girlfriend, who had recently embarked on a new life with a new man. We weren't spending time together or talking. It was too painful for me.

I was something more than lost. "Lost" is a blanket cliché for all manner of dissolute wanderings. Me, I was a refugee who'd barely survived a war zone, had fled from it, and then found himself a refugee all over again—this time from the very life he'd fled the war to live.

And I was angry—angry about what had happened to me, what had been taken from me, and angry that no one around seemed to accept how livid I was. "What is this guy's problem?" a lot of them seemed to be wondering. "He got well from leukemia, he's lucky to be alive, and he just seems pissed off that it happened to him in the first place." Sometimes people would come right out and say it.

"Well, yeah," is what I would say back.

I thought my feelings would be easy to relate to. If not among those who'd avoided catastrophe, at least by those who'd had some exposure to it. The lack of understanding I felt from both quarters made me angrier still. At the same time, I could see their point.

Anger is what I'd been hired to bring to my role in the play. The role of Doug consists of a series of diatribes against his father that top the milder scoldings the other "kids" give their parents. "You're an idiot!" Doug finally screams. "You're an idiot!"

I remember Jerry Zaks's one direction to me during rehearsals.

"That was good," he said. "Very good. You started at seven and went to ten.

"Now," he continued, "what if you start at ten?"

Doug's explosions resulted in huge roars of laughter from the audience and spontaneous eruptions of show-stopping applause. It surprised me at our first invited-audience dress rehearsal, and continued to occur at two junctures of every performance of the run. Taking it higher and higher every night, until I had nowhere left to go, was some of the purest fun I've ever had.

Another nightly event was a less pleasing ritual. Celebrities who'd seen the show flooded the backstage area after every *Six Degrees* performance. One after another they promenaded by: Meryl Streep, Steve Martin, Sidney Poitier. Katharine Hepburn, Richard Avedon, Lou Reed. One visitor was a guy I'd costarred with in the film *Taps* just a few years before I'd gotten sick. His name was Tom Cruise. While I was living in and out of hospitals, fighting just to stay alive, he'd opted to spend those same years becoming the biggest movie star in the world.

It wasn't the presence of the celebrities that irked me, or even the divergences in our fates. It was the same thing that had set me off at the dinner party years before. It was the compliments. They were abundant. They were heartfelt and sincere. And, since I was unrecognizable once I removed the wig I wore each night in the show, they were doled out to everyone but me.

The pack of six or seven of the younger cast members would gather our gear, hurrying toward whatever bar or restaurant we'd chosen as that night's destination. We'd work our way through the crowd toward the theater's exit, only to run into Ms. Streep or Ms. Hepburn. That night's royalty would embrace each of the other young actors, and turn their back on me.

"Oh, you're all so marvelous!" they'd coo. "I'd like to wrap you up and take you all home. You make me laugh so much!"

Sometimes one of my friends might try to intervene. "This is Evan," they'd say. "He was in the play, too."

"Really? Who did you play?"

"I was Doug."

No response.

"The kid in the window. Who calls his father an idiot . . . ? The scene when the whole audience bursts into applause . . . ?"

"The scene where . . . ? But . . . but . . . that boy had hair. That . . . that was you??"

By then they were so embarrassed that, instead of being generous with compliments, they generally needed consoling themselves. I was more embarrassed than they were, but I'd do my best to comfort them.

"That's all right. Don't worry about it."

I made light of it, but it tore me up. I was finally within millimeters of what I'd wanted for so long: professional recognition from those I admired. Except it wasn't "recognition," because no one recognized me.

There were times I even considered wearing the wig out after the show when I knew there was someone in the audience I wanted to meet. I never took that tack, but I did wear my "Evan Handler costume," as I took to calling the wig, to the party at Tavern on the Green celebrating our opening night on Broadway. It was the only way I knew to attend the event and enjoy the experience of being treated as a member of the cast.

Toward the end of the party the crowd had thinned out dramatically. The core of young actors was huddled close, barking made-up songs in tribal fashion as we each took turns stripping off portions of our elegant outfits. It became a ceremony of shedding the enforced formality of the event, of returning ourselves to the casual state we were more comfortable in. A few dozen other party guests were still spread around the room. My friends turned to face me and started to chant.

"Take it off! Take it off! Take it off! Take it off!"

I assumed they meant a tuxedo jacket or tie, but after hours of drinking and dancing, the adhesive from the wig tape was burning through the flesh of my neck. I reached up and peeled off the wig, back to front, as if scalping myself in reverse. There was a gasp, and all the singing stopped.

"Yea!!!" came the cheer from my friends, louder than I could have imagined. Some of the other lingering guests turned to look, but by then the group was vibrating like an amoeba again. It was as if they'd been set free by my gesture. Everyone was shrieking and dancing at twice the intensity of the second before. It was probably the first moment that I felt more authentic, and more accepted, with my naked head exposed than I did covered up.

THE LEUKEMIA DIAGNOSIS had slammed me five years earlier. The bone marrow transplant had been completed three years after that. I'd spent a full year recovering from that procedure and had been wading back into life for another year since. I was in a hit Broadway play. I had a passel of exhilarating new friends. I was classified as cured of the disease that had almost killed me and was considered to be something I hadn't been for five birthdays: *I was healthy.* But I wondered how long it might be before I'd be able to walk through the world without thinking back on those bad old days. I wondered when I might be able to skip the step of putting every experience I had into perspective by comparing it with how awful things had been back then. I was excited by thoughts of the future, a concept I hadn't had the pleasure of contemplating for half a decade. But I had the sense it was going to be a while before I again felt like a "normal" member of the human race.

I had no idea what an underestimation that time frame would prove to be.

Remember Richard Burr

I'VE TAKEN UP RUNNING. But I can't call myself "a runner." In fact, I can't really even claim that I run. What I do is trudge.

Every second or third day I walk swiftly from my home near the Hudson River into Central Park, where a dirt jogging track circles the reservoir embedded in the park's northern sector. I pass the seemingly homeless men who occupy the benches where I enter the park. One of the men—a muscular African-American—has recently taken to calling out greetings to me when I pass.

"Hey, lookin' good," he told me once.

"He looks better than me," is what I thought.

I'm the slowest man on the track. I'm also slower than the vast majority of the women. This includes, for the most part, the overweight and the elderly. I move at a speed that's hard to describe, because it's so slow it's hard to imagine. I've begun to wonder if the speed at which I walk *to* the park is greater than the speed at which I jog around the reservoir. I've also wondered if moving so slowly might actually use more energy than it would take to go faster. I have wondered, that is, until I try to speed up. I make it just once around the track—one point six or so miles—in utter agony, pleading with myself the whole way to stop, to keep going, to stop, to keep going. It's all I can do to keep from collapsing at the end of my single lap, while others trot past effortlessly for a third and fourth.

It's a problem, because I'm a competitive person. In fact, I'm so competitive it's rendered me unable to effectively compete. Even back in Little League, as a prepubescent baseball fanatic, my desire to excel was so strong that it created insurmountable anxiety. At practice I was a phenom. During games, I'd alternate between sensational plays and uncountable errors. I was Chuck Knoblauch before he was even born.

Now, when I go for my run, I can't stop comparing myself to everyone else on the track. About a quarter of the way in, I'll hear plodding footsteps from behind, see the shadow of a lumbering figure approach, and watch as a heavyset man makes his way into my field of vision. I'll privately mock the physical condition of this jogger, wondering how anyone could classify such a lethargic pace as cardiovascular conditioning, even as the person pulls astride and, eventually, passes me.

"God, he runs so slow," I'll think as I watch him pull ahead.

I RUN so slowly because I'm pacing myself. When it comes to physical exertion, I haven't got that good old-fashioned stamina. I have inner dialogues in which I tell myself that I'm now past forty, and for my age, I'm not doing so badly. After all, many of the people speeding by are under twenty-five. Except for the sixty-year-olds. That works a bit. Or I'll remind myself of where I've been: "How many of them have had bone marrow transplants?" I'll ask. "See how fast they run after that. See if they're standing upright."

I remember in junior high school, or sixth through eighth grade, we'd run a timed six-hundred-yard dash twice a year in gym class. A third of a mile. I could never understand why it was called a "dash," because, for me, it certainly wasn't. I was a decent athlete. I played baseball and basketball relentlessly with friends on local fields and courts. I even made my high school tennis team—though where I went to school, in 1978, tennis wasn't considered a "sport." It was classified as "recreation." The team didn't even have a photo in the school's yearbook. The football team was made up of thirty-five chunky local heroes of Irish and Italian descent. The tennis team had seven or eight members, at least half of whom were skinny Jewish potheads. On game days, football and basketball players wore their team jerseys to school, and all day long, kids called out in the halls, "Good game, Matt!" or "Go get 'em, Danny!" On the days we had tennis matches we'd wear our warm-up suits to school. Kids would give us funny looks as they passed, and ask "Why are you dressed like that?"

But the six-hundred-yard run was a dreaded event. It was usually announced the day before, which gave me twenty-four full hours to anticipate the pain and humiliation. I'd go about my business, getting absorbed by homework and my favorite television shows. Then, like the feeling I'd later come to know of waking up to remember my lover had just left me, thoughts of the next day's run would come barging back into my awareness. The next morning, dressed in my mildewed gym clothes and shivering in the post-dawn chill, I'd set off in the dewy grass, desperately trying to put distance between the feeblest of my classmates and myself. My speed was restricted by the limitations of my lungs. It would be only a matter of moments before they were burning, screaming at me to stop.

My proficiency in "the six hundred," as Mr. Cammaro, the gym teacher, called it, was poor. I usually finished toward the bottom third, right on the border between the last of those who thought it mattered and the ones who didn't give a shit. At least they acted as if they didn't. Who knows, maybe every one of them had dreams of athletic glory.

One kid I remember is Richard Burr, an utterly ostracized boy who walked the whole way. Richard would stare off into the sky, brushing his hand along the tops of the soft weeds that lined the trail, singing indecipherable tunes to himself as he drifted along. Some of the faster kids—the sadistic Nordic heartthrob Tom Skyfford, or the prematurely acne-infested but athletically gorgeous Jimmy Leiffert— who passed Richard on their second lap before he'd finished his first, would lightly smack the back of his head as they galloped by. Richard would make no move to evade their assaults. He'd stroll along, his face betraying nothing other than an assumption that some natural force had caused his head to snap forward every twelve seconds or so. Only when he'd fallen behind everyone would Richard now and then scamper a few paces. His gait was more of a skip than a sprint, and it wasn't to increase his speed. It wasn't because the gym teacher was watching. No, Richard fluttered along like a butterfly, his pace determined by nothing other than how much the wind and sun inspired him.

Did this mean that Richard Burr didn't dream of victory? Just because he'd given up all hope of excelling doesn't mean he didn't want to win. Or at least to avoid coming in last. But Richard was unreadable. Any shame he might have had as he ambled toward the finish line was invisible. Mr. Cammaro, on the other hand, was clearly insulted. He took his responsibility as a gym teacher seriously, keeping time even through the extra sixty or ninety seconds until Richard had rejoined the rest of the class. He'd issue Richard's time as a futile rebuke: "Six minutes, Richard!" Richard would simply collapse like a folding chair into the grass, just beyond the finish line. And when Mr. Cammaro blew his whistle (the gym teacher's equivalent to the *Kapo*'s sidearm) to begin the next activity, Richard always remained at a distance, tugging at weeds like an orphaned lamb feeding off to the side of the rest of the herd.

I was the anti-Richard. Being the youngest sibling in the family, and scrawny to boot, I'd been ultracompetitive since shortly after birth. In school, I couldn't bear the scorn of the other kids any more than I could stand Mr. Cammaro's disapproval. I had no ability, but I was determined to show heart. When I realized heart didn't improve my speed significantly, I just tried to avoid abasement. I'd stumble across the finish line, consumed with pain, aching for the two minutes or so to pass before my gasping would stop, and life would return to a relatively agony-free existence. Until the next semester's run. My status in the six hundred depended on how you looked at it. I was either the very best of the worst, or among the decent, but dead last.

And what was my time? How long would I be required to withstand the discomfort of exertion on that six-hundred-yard run? Two minutes twenty seconds? Four-forty? I don't remember. But how incongruous that lack of stamina seems when compared with my success in the super-marathon of chemotherapy and bone marrow transplantation I found myself running in my midtwenties. I'd never before thought of myself as a physically strong man. As an adult, I'd still never demonstrated any of the stamina I lacked in gym class as a kid. Yet, I managed to be one of the few left standing in the grueling hospital survival race. I suppose there are different types of endurance. I've skimmed some pages of the bicycle racer Lance Armstrong's book about his surviving testicular cancer that had spread to his lungs and brain, only to win the Tour de France seven consecutive times after his recovery. I haven't bought the book and read it—I'm much too competitive for that—but I have glanced through it. From what I've gleaned, Lance attributes much of his racing success to a willingness to endure more pain for longer periods of time than any of his opponents. It's why he believes his training is more effective, and why he's able to outlast others on the road. He also believes it's why he was able to absorb such large doses of the toxic chemicals that eradicated his cancer.

I must have had some of that same talent. But I'd never been aware of it before, and I haven't felt confident in it in all the years since, when I've been well. My memory of the six-hundred-yard dash, at twelve and thirteen years old, was that it hurt like hell. It either didn't hurt the others as much as it hurt me, or about two-thirds of them were more capable of enduring that pain than I was. Now that I'm up to three thousand yards it still hurts just as much. Not just physically. Even though there's no Mr. Cammaro there to scold those who might have walked part of the way, no Tom Skyfford or Jimmy Leiffert to feel jealous of for whipping along at speeds I couldn't have maintained for one-sixth the distance, I drag myself around that reservoir feeling as if the whole of my self-esteem depends on how long I last and how fast I go. As if everyone else on the track—the entire island of Manhattan—is watching and judging. After my run, I shuffle home feeling like a failure if I had to stop and rest anywhere along the way.

I'm not even out there to compete. I run for two reasons: to improve (hopefully) my health, and because it makes me feel better. You know, after I'm done. I get an endorphin rush and it alleviates, for a while, my tendency toward depression. But, in my mind, the comparisons with others continue. I'm not even sure anymore with whom I'm contending. The scolding is no longer coming from some small-town guy trying to make his living wrangling seventh-graders through meaningless physical fitness tests. Now it's coming from me. Maybe that's what makes me so uneasy, that no one's taking notice. I survived the eighth grade. Tom Skyfford and Mr. Cammaro didn't destroy me. I made it through high school, have ventured out into the world, earned a living where they tell you no one does, beat the odds on a terminal illness, reached my forties, and I'm moving one foot in front of the other, working my way down that track. Who cares if everyone else does it quicker and has an easier time? How come no one has offered me a prize?

What I've still got to learn is that it isn't about being given an ovation by the audience. After all this time, I still haven't quite gotten that it's about enjoying the run. The precious moments are the ones spent *on* the track, not the ones analyzing how quickly I got back off. The one who had it right was Richard Burr. He didn't let the clock, or the other kids, get in his way. He wasn't affected by Mr. Cammaro's admonishments. He looked at the sky, felt the sun on his cheek, picked a dandelion and blew the seeds, watched them scatter through the air and mingle with the bees. Richard wasn't in the game, as we knew it. He refused to play, except on his own. I always thought he must have felt tortured to always finish last, to have no chance at all of ever being the best, or even to count himself among them. I'd thought, for Richard, gym must have been hell. Looking back at eighth grade, or even last week, I wonder if that isn't where I've been keeping myself.

I don't know if Richard's wandering so freely today, or if his disinterest was completely unfeigned. But for me, as I enter the thirty-ninth grade, I'm going to try to strike a balance between pleasing myself and letting myself off the hook. Between wanting to push myself toward new and better things, and leaving myself free to wander through time as if the rest of humanity had no interest in me at all.

I've always looked at giving up hope as the end of life, and considering where I've been, I suppose that makes sense. But what if that's when life begins? When you become ready to release it. More of a Buddhist way of thinking about things, no? The freedom of no expectations. The joy of no desire. Of course, I don't know anything about Buddhism, so I don't know what I'm talking about. But I have a hunch it would be a good thing if I could get to a place where it doesn't matter if I run all the way around the park or never even make it there. Where it doesn't matter if I go faster than the two-hundred-pound woman or drop dead on the track. Where it's the journey that's important. Where the only thing that matters is whether I knew the sun loved me along the way.

The Sickest First Kiss

SOMEWHERE IN MY early to middle thirties I started, for the first time in my life, to date. I don't mean I'd never socialized with women before, or that I'd never had an acquaintanceship grow into something deeper. "Dating" is a term that means different things to different people, with most of the variations determined by context. To some it simply means spending time with prospective partners. To others it's the term used to describe an exclusive relationship. Still others use it as a euphemism for having sex. When I say that I started in my thirties "to date," what *I* mean is it was the first time in my life that I started to ask women out regularly, and to go on a succession of dates with a variety of them. I mean it's when I started to comparison shop.

I was feeling emboldened by several things, all of which concealed the fact that I had a serious lack of self-esteem. I'd been a professional actor for about fifteen years, had made a bit of a name for myself in the theater by appearing in seven Broadway shows before I turned thirty, and had gained even more notoriety by quitting several of them. The quitting streak was initiated by the first diagnosis of acute leukemia, which, in most circles, is considered unquestionable justification for leaving a job. A recurrence of the leukemia after I reappeared on Broadway led to the second quitting episode, not to mention some additional unwanted notoriety. However, the closest I got to fame was from quitting a Broadway play in mid-performance. That premature departure wasn't a result of serious illness: it was the result of being smacked across the ass with a three-foot stainless-steel sword by an alcoholic costar. The rules governing such resignations are murkier than those regarding multiple diagnoses of almost-always-fatal blood disorders. I suspect a few figures in the theater community found my rationalizations for leaving the stage that night to be less than compelling—though many did call to congratulate me and invite me out to lunches where I was encouraged to tell them the whole story. People love to hear everything you've got to say on a topic before they turn on you. My stretch of seven Broadway appearances occurred over a period of just eight years. The production I quit after being attacked was the last Broadway play I did, and that was more than seventeen years ago. But my performance was undeniably awful in that play. Maybe I haven't been hired since because, in that role, the theater world finally saw my limitations. Either that, or producers aren't crazy about a leading man who walks offstage in the middle of a show.

Anyway, I had gained some degree of notoriety. In the early nineties, not enough time had passed for my dubious reputation to become passé (which is a fancy word for "forgotten"). If I so chose, I was able to stop backstage at an off-Broadway show I'd enjoyed, ask to say hello to a heretofore unmet actress, and get a raised eyebrow of recognition upon uttering my name. Famous for all the wrong reasons is still famous. Broadway producers may have had qualms about hiring me, but the average working-class actor—each of whom had dreamed of running a sword through countless alcoholic costars of their own—saw me as a bit of a folk hero. It took two cases of leukemia and one dose of being smacked on the ass in front of five hundred people to find it, but I'd finally gotten my first taste of what I then took to be confidence.

This is the tactic I put to use to meet Nancy. Nancy is a beautiful blond actress whose performance, and appearance, had impressed me in a play on Forty-second Street's Theater Row. It was a gay-themed play, and Nancy portrayed a strong-willed, fiercely independent woman who glided effortlessly between a number of lovers. The dialogue was full of snappy ironic comments, and Nancy's performance was honest, bold, and sexy as hell.

In the theater's lobby after the show, the flirtatious and bawdy manner she carried back and forth between several groups of friends impressed me all the more. Nancy gave the impression of being a bit of a wild child. Or maybe I just projected that image onto her from her performance in the play. Though it's a cliché, the fact that the character she'd played had sexual relationships with both men and women only increased my ardor. If I can't actually *have* a bisexual girlfriend, I thought, I'd at least like to have a girlfriend who can portray one winningly.

After introducing myself, I spoke with Nancy briefly before leaving that night. The next day I returned to leave a note for her with the box office. I'm embarrassed to admit it (and with what I've already admitted, that's saying a lot), but I think I even made some kind of whimsical design out of the typewritten text of the invitation to get together. In spite of my heavy-handed tactics, Nancy called to arrange a date. When we reached the "What do you want to do?" portion of the phone call, Nancy didn't hesitate.

"I want to do something you've always wanted to do but have never done with anyone before."

That sounded like quite an invitation. But just because my mind leaped to sexual escapades involving myself and anywhere from one to a couple of dozen others, that didn't mean that's what Nancy had intended to suggest.

"Well . . . I've always wanted to ride the Staten Island Ferry," I said. And so it was settled.

It wasn't as timid a suggestion as it seems. Or maybe it was. But it wasn't absent of romantic intent. I'd heard from scores of people over the years that riding the Staten Island Ferry at night was one of the great romantic experiences New York City had to offer. When I mentioned to a few friends my plans for a first date with an actress I'd just met, I got nods of approval in which innocence played no part. Judging from some of those smirks, I could have assumed I was in for the make-out session of my life—if not a hefty dose of barely concealed public sex—all in exchange for the fifty-cent round-trip fare.

Date night arrived, and Nancy and I met at a Japanese restaurant for a quick snack. It was already late, as Nancy was still working in the play and had finished her eight P.M. performance. We then rode the subway to South Ferry, the closest station to the Staten Island Ferry dock. It was a cold autumn night, a Friday, already close to midnight. Instead of finding late-night revelers or spent partiers making their way home, the subway below Fourteenth Street held what seemed like a crowd of commuters. Business suits and corporate skirts dominated. Briefcases and portfolios boarded at stop after stop. But there was something slightly off-kilter about those nine-to-five folks. When we reached the last stop there was a rush-hour-like scramble as everyone hurried off the train toward the boat terminal. Looking up at the schedule board, Nancy and I realized we were within seconds of missing one of the last late-night ferries. We hurried through turnstiles, rushed up an enormous gangplank, and boarded the back of the boat.

The ferry was crowded, but we didn't discover that right away. We hovered on the back deck, watching the lights of Manhattan recede. It wasn't even a deck, really—more a cold, slippery metal platform at the base of a circular stairway leading to the chained-off upper regions of the boat. It was just Nancy and myself and a few other brave stragglers outdoors that night. We leaned against wooden railings and gazed at the eruption of man-made structures shrinking behind us. For a few frigid minutes, with the smell of diesel fuel and the spray of polluted harbor water tickling our senses, Nancy and I experienced the romantic splendor of the Staten Island Ferry. Finally, chased indoors by the chill, we walked a narrow, warped, red-floored corridor into the main hold of the ship.

THE SUDDEN WARMTH was startling. It wouldn't have been unpleasant without the dampness that accompanied it. It was like entering a locker room after the team's shower. The large hold's center was filled with rows of chairs and benches, and more benches lined the perimeter of the room. All the seats were filled with people. These were the same people we'd ridden with on the subway, only joined by a lot more like them. Men and women in Burberry scarves and trench coats. People accompanied by attaché cases.

The uniforms we don unconsciously come suddenly into harsh relief when surrounded by those who wear a different one from us. Walking in midtown Manhattan, I rarely pay attention to what others are wearing, and I rarely feel anyone taking notice of me. But there on the ferry it was clear that Nancy and I were interlopers, dressed differently, perhaps even living differently, than those around us. And in one of those shifts of perception that makes you wonder how you'd missed what you're now seeing, I realized Nancy and I were separated from our fellow passengers in one other respect: we were sober.

There must have been three hundred people inside the boat, all of them something less cheerful than drunk. They were two or three hours *past* being drunk. Meaning they were still drunk, but they were now away from their friends, they were now queasy, and they were now at sea.

Young women were passed out, their mouths gaping, splayed legs stretching drooping pantyhose to their limits. They were wearing sneakers and had dress shoes poking out of their neglected backpacks. The skirts of several were skewed, zippers facing forward or sideways, as if they'd been groped over the course of the evening and had fled quickly, with no time to straighten up. Several of the men, foggy-eyed if awake at all, were dwarfed by mounds of plastic-wrapped dry cleaning they'd picked up in preparation for the next workweek, the crispness of the fresh clothes accentuating the disarray of everything around them. Staggering men slipped on spilled beer as they made their way back from the concession stand. Documents fell onto the wet floor from the laps of unconscious executives. The smell of hot dogs mixed with stale beer and bad breath. Women snored as loudly as men, as if finally free, in sleep, from the comparative constraints of their workweek existence.

"We've stumbled upon a ritual," I whispered to Nancy. "Look. It's 'The Retreat of Friday Night's Defeated.' These are the people who didn't get picked up by anyone. Who don't live in Manhattan. Who *have* to get home. The ones who still live with their parents." Two strangers' heads flopped toward each other. They nuzzled briefly, then shifted away.

I looked to my right and immediately wished that I hadn't. A young man in his twenties, dressed in the ubiquitous blue suit, was on the verge of getting ill. He was as disheveled as the others, tie undone, shirt wrinkled, sweat stains in all the appropriate places. I'm not sure if my fascination would have been as complete if he'd been more alert, but he was alternately nodding off, then snapping awake with each wave of nausea. Eventually, the queasiness sobered him somewhat, and his eyes registered a brief hint of alarm. He looked surprised, rocked himself back and forth, trying, apparently, to appease the beast eager to escape from within. We were pulling toward the Staten Island dock, and the queasy young executive stood, keen to disembark.

Then I saw what I saw. Still to this day I wish I hadn't. It was one of those things that are so vivid, so visceral, that you know the memory will be with you as long as you live, as if you'd experienced the sensations yourself. A wave of nausea took the young executive by surprise. His cheeks puffed out and his lips clamped shut. He froze, mouth full. He looked furtively once to his left, once to his right, chewed twice, and swallowed. He stood slack-jawed, a mixture of relief and confusion on his face. The way a fighter looks on the canvas after being knocked down, the worst having come and gone. He wiped his mouth with the back of his hand, then stared dumbly at his skin, examining whatever he'd smeared there.

Watching his struggle was only the first in a series of mistakes. The second was looking back to Nancy. As soon as I met her eyes I knew she'd witnessed the same thing I had. Still, I found myself starting to form the question.

"Did you—"

"Yes," she interrupted. And we didn't speak again until we were off the boat.

The next mistake was getting off the boat at all. Before we knew it, the ferry pulled away, heading back toward the island of opportunity across the water. Nancy and I found ourselves in the grimness of Staten Island's Staten Island Ferry terminal, with more than an hour to kill before the next boat would depart. We walked outside thinking we might find something to explore, but all we could make out was an expanse of parking lot stretching into the distance. Beyond that was darkness.

We wandered back into the terminal, taking in the surroundings for the first time. They weren't cheering. The room was bathed in fluorescent light so bright I thought it might deep-fry food. The waiting room wasn't full, but it wasn't empty, either. Scattered on benches and the floor were homeless people and drunks; junkies, punks, and punk junkies; goth teens and their pets; and various other life-forms that were neither advanced nor owned by those claiming to be. Our first date had come to a crushing halt in a dank holding cell. We were the only travelers, surrounded by those who had nowhere else to go.

I then made the ultimate mistake of the evening. I somehow convinced myself it would be an impressive gesture if I were to lean over and kiss her. Right there. Within the vector of heat wafting off the rank bodies. Such defiance, I thought. After all we'd seen together that night, what an assertion of our good health, our good fortune. What a demonstration of the power of her appeal. The fact that even Calcutta-like conditions could not transcend my desire. The perversity will make me seem so . . . *dashing.* I was oblivious to what the real lure was. Forget what the atmosphere proved about Nancy's appeal to me. If I could get her to accept my kiss in the midst of the homeless, the drug-addicted, and the peculiarly pierced, imagine what that would mean in terms of *my* appeal to *her.* The real motivation in kissing Nancy in the Staten Island Ferry terminal was to conquer my doubts about the desirability of *me.*

I gazed at Nancy a moment too long. I leaned over and placed my lips on hers. We kissed, and we kissed again. We kissed for some minutes. I thought about all the things that had led me to kiss her there, and I even whispered some of them to her. But it didn't work. In the long run it was okay. We dated for a few weeks and had some good times. (Then again, that's not really "the long run," is it? Okay, in the medium run.) But there in the terminal of the Staten Island Ferry, at the end of a long workweek, in a city where a room, a facility, a building, a borough, can absorb all the exhaustion of its million or more inhabitants, we kissed, and it was nothing but disgusting. The gesture might have been impressive, but it was inappropriate. The conditions might not have transcended my desire, but my desire didn't transcend anything.

Nancy smiled a wan smile and pulled away. We sat in silence for the next hour, embarrassed by our heartiness and privilege, and waited for the boat that would take us back to Manhattan. Where beauty and hope, brutality and destitution, possibility and limitations, coexist in quantities large enough to be selectively ignored by those who choose to do so. I'd rather not admit it, but I must be one of them. Because that was ten years ago, and I never rode the Staten Island Ferry again.

I Don't Know

S TEVEN SILVERSTEIN committed suicide when he was seventeen years old and a senior in high school. I was fifteen, two years behind. I don't know why he did it, and I don't know how, though the method I heard of involved a car with a flexible tube threaded through a window from the vehicle's exhaust pipe. But there was no way to be sure. There was no proof. No witness to the fact. The word just spread.

I always pictured Steven in the car at night, parked on the chopped-up, rarely used private roads that wove around the dilapidated Pine Lake summer bungalows across the street from his house. These roads weren't even supposed to be accessible from Furnace Dock Road, the main artery through the wooded area where the Silversteins and my family both lived. There were two entrances from Furnace Dock to the Pine Lake cabins, and each had a worn, thin chain that sagged between two cockeyed, rusty, hollow metal posts. The chain draped mostly on the ground, making passage as easy as if it weren't there. But in 1976, the simple fact of its existence was enough to keep most people from crossing over. We kids walked past the chains all the time. To jump the fence and use the always-empty red clay tennis courts. To play basketball on a cracked, weed-strewn court hidden high up the desolate hill. To get out of sight and smoke a joint. But cars didn't tread those roads out of season. The tire tracks and patchy asphalt were barely distinguishable from the woods and fields on either side. This hidden cobwebbed collection of ancient summer recreation is where I always imagined Steven Silverstein to have died. But I don't know.

I DIDN'T KNOW Steven well, or his sister Reva, who was a year or so younger than I. But we had many friends in common. One of Steven's closest friends was Russell, the oldest of the Lesh brothers, who lived down the street. Ron Lesh, the middle brother of the three, was my best friend. Russell wasn't only my friend Ron's big brother, though. He was also the official boyfriend of seventeen-year-old Linda Huff, the girl who would come to my house to kiss me for hours on my bed before going down the street to have sex with Russell. I don't know why Linda never had sex with me. She said she didn't want to do the seducing. I don't know if that was the real reason. And I don't know why I was too shy and scared to take what was being offered. I just don't know.

I remember gathering at the Lesh house a day or two after news of Steven's death spread through the high school. That's the way it happened back then. There was no announcement or school assembly. No grief counselors offered support to shaken students. The only confirmation of the truth of the rumor was that no adults denied it. And Steven wasn't there.

Steven's sister Reva was ushered in and out of the house, her head bowed and silent. Stan Dorsk, a huge, already graduated black sheep of the basketball team and one of Steven's good friends, bent low to enter mournfully and mumble before walking out again. Stan was a clearly unhappy young adult, with a violent temper that flared whenever he was drunk, which was almost every night. It was Stan who ended up closest to Reva. They each took their connection to Steven, fused it onto the other, and became the oddest of couples. Stan, six foot six and almost twenty years old. Reva, five feet tall and all of fourteen. They became inseparable—stoned, stone-faced companions in mourning. Their union was scandalous at the time, and probably thrived for that reason. Whatever rage Reva might have held toward her parents and their possible role in her brother's destruction was, I would think, soothed by giving herself over to a depressed giant who drank himself fat and brawled often in the two years since he'd left high school. As for Stan, when asked about Reva's tender age, he simply burped and said, "If they're old enough to sit at the table, they're old enough to eat."

In the days after Steven died, a steady flow of older schoolmates continued at the Lesh house. The house had always been a central gathering point for various clumps of high schoolers due to the relative lack of parental supervision, or even—as most of the other kids understood the term—parental concern. It was the house where a Lesh brother could close the door to his room with a girl inside and count on not being disturbed. It was the house where pot smoking was allowed indoors. For better or for worse, the Lesh house was the place where fifteen- to nineteen-year-olds could congregate and interact with little fear of interference. Where they could be true to their purest natures.

This freedom from adult influence allowed its own strict hierarchy to develop, with rungs of privilege often determined by nothing more than grade level. In the days and nights after Steven died, there were closed doors and myriad conversations to which Ron and I were not privy. There were sounds of sobbing, and teenagers reappeared red-faced. Linda Huff, the girl I loved, closed the door to Russell's bedroom—just off the living room, where we all tended to gather—and his brothers and I tried to make believe we weren't hearing him cry.

Jesus, this is awful, I thought. But, for me, it was better than the usual, which was listening to them fuck.

As for what they all talked about, whether Steven left a note, who felt angry or who felt hurt, who felt guilty or who was secretly pleased, I don't know.

MICHAEL GOULD WAS a kid my age, and he died in ninth or tenth grade. The story was he slept out in his tree house with his best friend Paul Santino. When Paul went inside to go to the bathroom, Michael knocked over the kerosene lamp in his sleep and burned up with the tree. I remember Michael and Paul as the kids who used to call me a fag and laugh in Mr. Bowles's science class.

Tammy Albanese was killed by a car while riding her horse on the road the summer after eighth grade. A few months before, I'd caught her defacing posters I'd put up in my campaign for student government president.

I didn't know how to feel about the deaths of these kids who'd behaved badly toward me. I hadn't wished them dead. I didn't feel vindicated. While I was shocked, I wasn't particularly sad. I didn't know if any of the stories about how they died were true, or if they were even really dead. I had no reason to doubt it, other than its incomprehensibility. But I didn't really *know*. And I always wondered if Tammy's horse was killed as well, or if somehow it survived. What happened to Steven Silverstein's car? Was it sold? Given away? Destroyed? I don't know.

Kevin Gheen was my friend from ten years old. He died when he was about thirty, climbing mountains in France. Shortly after I heard about Kevin's death, I saw Ron Lesh, who'd also known him, for the first time in some years and he asked, "Do you know what the story is with Kevin? Do you know how it happened?" Ron and I were eating pizza and talking about turning forty, him married with two kids and me single all over again.

"No," I said. "I don't know."

Rema Hort was a friend, and she died, too. Cancer. Thirty years old. My cousin Greg, maybe thirty-five, of AIDS. Jeff Lowenthal, one of my earliest agents, one of the first to go from that illness. Brother Jonathan Ringcamp, Andie Lui, Willie Dingle. Twenty-three to forty, each one. Martin Herzer. A. J. Antoon. Gary Petrillo. So many of them have been gone now for so long. Where did they go? Why did they go when they did? Why didn't I? I don't know.

BECAUSE OF MY history of illness and recovery, I started getting asked my views on complex issues when I was only about twenty-five. A young age for philosophizing about life and death, even for a theologian. Sometimes the questions would come from friends, but often from mere acquaintances. The inquisitors might be my age, or two or three generations older. Do you think things happen for a reason? I'd be asked. Do you think you can alter your own destiny? Does prayer really work? Do you think life has a meaning? Is there a higher power?

I don't know.

A very common question, when I was a kid, was whether or not you believed in God. It came up all the time, and it was used as a kind of introductory identity test. Almost like asking a stranger from what tribe they hailed, the question flew in quick succession to several other standards.

"What religion are you?"

"You like the Yankees or Mets?"

"How long can you hold your breath?"

"Do you believe in God?"

I've always had an odd relationship to that last question. For me, the answer has always seemed straightforward and inevitable, and it's always been the same. I don't know. I just don't know.

I don't mean that in a passive sense. I don't mean it as a cop-out from contemplation. I've tried to live my life from a position of being open to all possibilities, with great curiosity and wonder over what, to me, can never be known. To the possibility that there is meaning beyond what's easily seen; to the possibility that there's not. To the possibility that there is some form of intelligence guiding the intricate systems that sustain us, and to the possibility that there's not. But if you're going to ask me what I think the situation *is*, when I close my eyes at night and dream, wondering if I'll get to wake up again, or if it matters whether I do or not, then you'll hear what, to me, is the most sensible refrain: I don't know.

I am fascinated by our conundrum as humans living on planet Earth. I've said to friends, probably more times than they've wanted to hear, "We live in outer space. Do you know that? Can you believe it? *We live in outer space.*" It's a crucial thing to remind myself, because it justifies and enhances my choice to remain committed to philosophical noncommitment. We do not know where we live. We have no idea of our own address. As many maps as have been produced, with all the stellar observations and radio frequency surveillance, we have no idea what substance contains us, where it came from or where it's headed, if it has a purpose or what it might be, how it started, or how long it will last. We do not know. Whether we admit it readily or not, the most advanced of our species are, in relation to the universe beyond our planet, identical to tribes that have no conception of the world beyond their rain forest.

I don't mean to endorse atheism. I embrace that point of view no more than the idea of a deity. My favorite argument in favor of a guiding force came from my brother when I was seventeen. I was involved in my first sexual relationship with my first requited love, Noreen.

When somehow the topic came up, my brother surprised me by declaring, "Of course there's a God, Evan. Why do you think your thing fits inside hers? You think that's an accident?"

That gave me pause.

But I've remained a fairly "I don't know" guy. Not in the passive, desultory manner most would imagine. I've made a conscious, emphatic decision to remain undecided.

I ONCE HEARD a story told by a songwriter who'd had a new composition criticized by a peer. "He hated it," the songwriter said. "*Hated* it! He told me he thought it was maudlin and sentimental."

The songwriter's reply was splendid. "Well," he said. "All I can tell you is that it came from an extremely heartfelt place."

It's a perfect response, I thought upon hearing it. It takes all questions of quality, and even taste, away. It brings the discussion back to the heart and soul of the writer, who has communicated both his pleasure at having been true to himself as well as his commitment to his point of view. "It came from an extremely heartfelt place."

I feel a great kinship with his philosophy. When it comes to the questions I've been asked about suffering and existence, about patterns versus chaos; when it comes to life and death, or light and dark; when I think about Steven Silverstein, or Michael Gould, or Tammy Albanese; my friends Kevin and Rema or my cousin Greg; Jeff Lowenthal, Brother Jonathan, Andie Lui, Willie Dingle, Martin Herzer, Gary Petrillo, and A. J. Antoon. The millions who've died early, suffered unjustly, or been inexplicably blessed. Why others succumbed and I escaped, or a plane crashes killing hundreds while Mr. Smith decided not to fly.

Do I think there's a God? I don't know. A reason we're here? I don't know. Is there a spirit that survives, or do we disappear? I don't know.

I don't know.

I don't know.

It's not that I don't wonder, I just don't know.

But what I can tell you is this: I don't know from an extremely heartfelt place.

The Biggest Mistake I Ever Made, or "I Don't"

O N VALENTINE'S DAY in the year of 1999 I proposed marriage.
My girlfriend Patricia and I had planned to cook dinner together
that night, as well as bake a cake for dessert. We'd never cooked
well together before—had hardly even tried, in fact—but we were set
to start with a challenging pan-fried cod from the Union Square
Cafe cookbook. The idea of the cake came from a newly purchased
appliance. For Christmas, several weeks earlier, I had bought us a
shiny new five-and-a-half-quart-capacity KitchenAid mixer. Fire-
engine red.

I've owned only one car in my life. It was also red, a brand-new
Acura Integra that was bought for me by my father. We weren't
wealthy, and my father had never before bought me any item
approaching the expense of a car. He hadn't even paid that much for
my college. For that expense I'd taken out my own student loans. But
the car was on Dad, because I was twenty-seven years old and conva-
lescing from a bone marrow transplant with only a twenty-five per-

cent chance of ever seeing thirty. The checkbook comes out mighty quick when death hangs in the air.

The only reason I mention the car is that it was also red. Well, that, and that it brings up the fact that I might have been dying at the time. It's important to work that information into any story I tell, in the hope it might excuse whatever behavior I confess to later on. And after two bouts with leukemia, four brutal rounds of conventional chemotherapy, two bone marrow harvests, and a bone marrow transplant, I just can't seem to ever stop talking about the illness anyway. Did I mention it was twenty years ago?

The KitchenAid mixer was red and so was the car. This is the story of how I proposed to Patricia, using the cake we baked together on Valentine's Day in the year of 1999. It's important to note, though, that I'd also proposed to Jackie, the girlfriend I'd had throughout the illness, and afterward when I owned the car. Did I mention that it was also red? And that the mixer was, too?

Still, I don't consider myself to have been engaged twice. The first marriage proposal happened while I was sick, during an especially grim passage of that particularly bleak period. "Deathbed marriage proposal" is a term that fits in every way, other than that I didn't actually go ahead and die. I was, though, in a bed, in a hospital—Memorial Sloan-Kettering Cancer Center, to be exact—with an infection and tubes running into and out of me and, well, if one can get any closer to dying and going to Hell, I don't know about it, and I don't want to. You see, there were *extenuating circumstances.* In that particular instance, for that particular indiscretion, I had an *excuse.* I may rely on it too much, you may think I use it as a crutch; I may have woven it into the myth I've made out of my life and attributed all sorts of preexisting neuroses to it. But it did happen, I'm trying to get over it, and if you're ever jealous of the way I occasionally use it to bludgeon others into submission, then I suggest you start in on the sixteen years of psychotherapy that have been so marginally successful for me.

As I've said, the car was red, and so was the KitchenAid mixer. Or, the car was red, and the KitchenAid mixer still is, because it still sits on my kitchen counter. It has been used only once since baking that cake back in 1999 and that was to make mashed potatoes, because they are one of Patricia's favorite foods. The mixer gleams in the light and projects a splendid image. It is impressive to visitors and conjures assumptions of skill, precision, and power. It sits in my house, a useless item that is rarely touched or noticed, and in all those ways that red KitchenAid mixer is just like me. It was bought to impress my lost love Patricia, as the red car was chosen to impress the fiancée before. I no longer live with either of them, but share my space with a cold, indifferent, yet beautiful machine. I wonder when it will decide to leave me as well.

The baking of the cake went well. Patricia and I put aside some of the difficulties we'd had, to that point, when trying to do things as a team. I say the difficulties "we'd" had, but the problems were really mine. I have extremely low tolerance for anyone doing anything in any way that I don't think of as being the best way. (If you're starting to find me tiresome, please remember that I was once very sick.)

I was in love with Patricia. Which would only be appropriate, being the night I asked her to marry me. I had my plan mapped out, but kept it secret from her. We baked the cake, and I tried to be a better man than I was. I tried not to take over in the kitchen, not to find fault with her inexperience as a cook, not to instruct her on things she didn't ask to learn, and not to show how much it bothered me that she didn't want to learn more. (Oops. It just showed again.)

When the cake was done, we decorated it. Patricia used a kit I'd bought, and she drew, with icing, the most perfect, beautiful multicolored flowers I'd ever seen. Drawing is a talent I've never had and never will, and as she was doing it, I felt all the wonder that a person is supposed to feel about people they admire. Patricia was the most sensational, lovely, warm, fun, and enjoyable person on earth to me that night, and I was amazed at how calm I was about what I was about to do.

I sent Patricia out of the kitchen after the cake was done. Our plan was to put the cake aside while we cooked our fish, and then to eat it for dessert. But I told Patricia that I had a surprise, and would need a few minutes alone before we cooked dinner. She left the kitchen, only slightly suspicious, and I took up the tools with which she'd already decorated the cake. I chose a bright red icing—no intent behind it at the time, I'm noticing the symmetry only now—and I wrote on the cake in a billowy script: "Happy Valentine's Day. Will You Marry Me?" I put the cake out of sight, on top of the refrigerator, and we cooked and ate our fish. We had a wonderful dinner. Afterward, I presented the cake to Patricia, who burst into tears and said, "Yes." The night was the high point of my life in terms of trust, faith, certainty, and lack of ambivalence. I was, for sure, the best man that I ever had been.

I have a videotape of my marriage proposal. Not the actual moment, but the ones immediately after. There are images of Patricia and myself blowing kisses at each other, teary-eyed, glowing with love. I was struck, when I first viewed them, by how bad we looked. Not in any serious way, just the lack of pretension and preparation. We were dressed in sweatpants and stained, faded T-shirts—the kind you only wear to sleep, or to lie around the house in. The kind you only let your lover see you in.

There is something tender and unnerving about the casualness of the people in that video. There is something incongruous about my droopy pants and T-shirt with peeling lettering. Patricia's smile beams from an unwashed face under crushed, uncombed hair. It is either an image of marvelously unself-conscious contentment and acceptance, or another symptom of how dreadfully I took her devotion for granted.

Now Patricia is gone. Our engagement lasted two years before flaming out. That's the same amount of time we'd been together prior to that Valentine's night, though the second half of our relationship wasn't nearly as much fun as the first. Two good years, two bad. We spent as much time trying to turn each other into things we weren't as we did enjoying ourselves.

Also gone are Jackie, Graciella, Ellie, Rebecca, Christina, and Noreen. Not all fiancées, thank God, but somewhat serious relationships each. In between there were less devoted liaisons, and still more encounters that, I'll confess, were not always in between. (Remember, I was sick . . .) Does it seem insane that I consider myself, generally speaking, to be a pretty decent guy? Apparently several of my exes agree. Of the list above, three have remained among my dearest long-term friends.

Patricia isn't the first partner I've had trouble loving properly in person, only to be overwhelmed by a surge of feelings after she's gone. I'm onto the pattern. And it's only taken me four decades to decipher it. My father thinks it's simply a sign of the times, bless his soul. He finds it bewildering, and confesses that he can't relate. "I've never had a broken heart," he said to me after one painful breakup of mine. At that moment I realized we'd never be able to truly know each other. "Your generation has too many options," he said. But the vast majority of my friends were in stable marriages with children. It was his son who had such difficulty choosing.

MY TEN-YEAR-OLD NEPHEW was, in his way, more compassionate by way of being more direct. His understanding was limited, due to his years, but his questions and comments could not have been cannier.

"Why did you and Patricia break up, Uncle Evan?" he asked. I'd felt bad as this visit approached—my first without Patricia—because I knew my nephews and niece were fond of her and loved the way she played with them for hours at a time. I wanted to let him know that it was important to recognize your mistakes, as well as to help him avoid some of the mistakes I'd made.

"I wasn't very nice to her, Josh," I said. "You ever have a friend who wasn't very nice to you and so you don't want to play with him anymore?"

"So, it was your fault?" he asked.

"Yep. It was my fault."

Josh cocked his head and arched his eyebrows. He looked over at his mother first—my sister, and his teacher in life—then looked back at me. He scrunched up his mouth and shrugged his shoulders and said, "Well, if it was your fault . . ." There was no need to say any more.

So what's a guy like me to do? One who feels love so deeply, but only after the object of it is gone? And what do I do with a videotape of a broken engagement? Throwing it out, or taping over it, seems a sacrilege. It was—in some ways it *is*—the proudest moment of my life. I have tapes of Patricia and me hiking in the woods, hunting for houses, and promising to love each other forever, through anything. Is a dream a lie if it doesn't come true? For now, the tapes are in a drawer with the love notes and letters I can't bear to destroy. They sit inside my desk, aging like bottles of fine wine, potential betrayers to any current visitors of the depth of my regret and sorrow.

THE PATH IS not so grim as I've made it out to be. I've already been slightly involved with another woman (I don't blame you if you want to tell her to run), a fiercely intelligent Australian whom I'd thought might possess qualities to give us a better shot at making a go of it than those I've been with before. By that I mean she's not quite so cowed by me. As I rant and rave, complain, or—as she puts it—"whinge and moan," she doesn't indulge me or try to placate me. She doesn't go out of her way to ease my easily aroused discomfort. She tends to briefly interrupt whatever she's doing, look my way, and say, "Could you . . . could you *stop*? Could you just *stop*?" And lo and behold, I do. I've discovered that I can, and so I do. The fact that she lives 12,500 miles away also seems to help us get along.

I've recently passed my fortieth birthday, so the "just stop" realization may be way past due. Forty years is a long time to learn some basic lessons about restraint and tolerance in relationships. Still, I'm happy it arrived just the same. It means there's hope for me yet, so long as I live long enough.

And since forty was a birthday I thought I'd never see (I just had to work that in one more time), who knows how much time I might still have to get it right? I think the first step was being able to know what my nephew picked up on, and it's what I'd say to Patricia today if she'd listen to me. It was my fault, Patricia. You were my friend, and I didn't treat you right. It was my fault.

But I suppose she already knows that.

Menace to Society

I'VE BROKEN UP twenty-seven times. Not only do I disagree with
the song about it being hard to do, I've found it's impossible to
avoid.

That twenty-seven is an amazing number when you consider that
those breakups have been spread over only ten women. That's an
average of 2.7 breakups per relationship. Since I have ended some
relationships cleanly, that means I've had other relationships within
which the breakups have numbered four, five, six, or even seven.
Lucky seven.

You'd think one's greatest failures and successes would occur in
separate arenas. If one were to excel in cooking, say, one might expect
to fail in, oh, civil engineering. I wouldn't anticipate that the chef who
dazzles with a flawless Chilean sea bass bathed in lemongrass-
coconut broth might fall flat on his face with scrambled eggs. I, however, have somehow managed to combine my greatest successes and
failures into the same category: women.

I had my first sexually loaded kiss at fourteen. The girl's name was Joanna, and we were seventeen days into a four-week American Youth Hostels bicycle trip. Joanna had been open until then about her interest in Brett, a sixteen-year-old member of the group. Brett was six feet tall, a sharp-jawed, straight-haired, chiseled piece of teenage dreamdom. I was five foot four, weighed barely a hundred pounds, and had a tangled mess of wildly uncombed hair. Over the course of our six-hundred-mile journey, I was mistaken for a girl more often than my new girlfriend.

But Brett was a trifle odd. He'd started boasting, about one week out on the road, that he hadn't showered since setting off from Manhattan—and that he didn't intend to until he was back home again. Our entire trip was scheduled to last thirty days, and Brett kept his word.

It took Joanna seventeen days to change her mind. I'll never know what would have happened had Brett decided to bathe after sixteen. But Joanna and I were never really a "couple." Even our late-night, sleeping-bags-next-to-each-other-on-the-church-floor make-out sessions were surreptitious, illegal by American Youth Hostels standards. On the nights we camped out in tents, both her tent-mate and mine offered to do the old switcheroo to allow us a night of what would have been, to me, inconceivable pleasure. I have no idea whether Joanna was eager to accept or not, or whether she was disappointed by my inability to imagine her desire as equal to mine. I just know I was thrilled that the cute Jewish girl from Long Island found my scrawny, unkempt self sexy at all. A few secret wet kisses when no one was looking were more than I'd come to expect on that summer bike trip.

I actually liked Joanna's friend Tracy more than I liked her. Tracy's the one who had been the object of my fantasies since we'd set off two weeks earlier. When she approached and asked if I liked Joanna (the eighth-grade method of being asked out on a date), I figured Tracy wasn't interested. I felt lucky that at least one of them was, and, instead of saying, "Well, yeah, but I like you better," I settled for what I could get. The first telling inaction in a life of romantic missteps.

My first real girlfriend, my first sexual partner, was Noreen. We started dating when I was seventeen and just out of high school. Just to show that I don't give up and leave relationships easily, Noreen started things off shortly after we started seeing each other by having sex with my older brother. Then she told me about it. I'm not endorsing this strategy, but I stayed with her for another year after that. Only when she told me that the two of them had done it again did I break things off with her clean as a whistle. One relationship, one breakup. One for one. I'm not sure how, or on what grounds, you break up with your brother, though.

IT TOOK A YEAR or two before I'd recovered enough to try again. I was nineteen and a student living in the East Village when Graciella and I met. Graciella was twenty-five and an aspiring actress who earned her living as a waitress. It was with Graciella that I began my experimentation with repetitive breakups. We were together, off and on, for four years. When we finally split for good, after five or six false stops, I was twenty-three and an established off-Broadway actor. I even had a couple of Broadway and film credits to my name. Graciella was twenty-nine and still a waitress. I suffered, and made her suffer, from an irresistible desire to coexist with someone who felt more like a peer, coupled with a fear that no one else would ever love me as much as she did. As soon as I met someone who seemed as if she might, I dropped Graciella cold.

I remember the final scene with her clearly. We'd already survived the dreadful "see a bit less of each other" episodes, and had even passed through the euphemistic "date other people" period. Still, after emotional rejection and sexual infidelity, the connection survived. When I was sure I had to go, and when telling her I'd met someone else I was interested in and wanted to pursue wasn't enough to unseal the deal, I fouled the waters in the only irreparable fashion I knew. I told Graciella the truth: I said that, while I thought she had oodles of gifts to offer, I didn't think they were in the arena of acting. I told her I didn't think she had the talent to get what she wanted in that world, and that I thought she was cheating herself out of potential happiness and fulfillment by continuing in her unrequited quest.

Graciella told me that if I didn't respect her as an actress then I couldn't respect her as a human being. She announced that she wouldn't stay with me even if I changed my mind. "Oh, and by the way. Remember when my ex-boyfriend Ryan was in town two years ago and stayed over and I told you we didn't have sex? Well, I lied."

It's disturbing to learn you've been deceived, even when you've decided you're through with a relationship. I took Graciella's exiting jab as evidence I was making the right decision. Years later, when I learned she was living happily in New Jersey working as a master yoga instructor, I took it as evidence I was right about her acting talent, too.

THE WOMAN I left Graciella for is named Jackie. Just weeks after we'd moved in together, after being a couple for a year, I was diagnosed with acute leukemia and told that my life was almost certainly over. Jackie remained my girlfriend and supporter during years of navigating the treacherous terrain of drastic medical treatments. I've already said more about our relationship in print than anyone ever wanted to hear to begin with. Suffice it to say that she's the one I broke up with seven times—if not more. The final split was sixteen years ago, and she's been my closest friend ever since. I guess it pays, when ending a relationship, to really be sure.

This sad recap has already brought us into my thirties. I suppose my precocious professional success, as well as my four-year stint with a woman six years my senior, shielded me from recognizing my often infantile behavior. It was only in the midst of my next attempt at a relationship, and its multiple breakups, that I had the first inklings of my own immaturity. I met and began seeing a woman named Ellie, and things seemed for a time to be stable. I felt, amazingly enough, relatively content. There were the rather routine nights when I'd wake up at three in the morning to find her crying in another unlit room, but she'd assure me that it had nothing to do with me or us, and that crying regularly alone in the dark at three A.M. didn't really mean any-thing anyway. I accepted her explanations, figuring if she couldn't share her worries with me, I wouldn't make them my problem. I then developed an infatuation with an actress I was working with who liked nothing better than fucking other women's boyfriends and husbands, and I started the grueling process of breaking up with Ellie and changing my mind so many times that she finally shoved me out her door for good. But things were—all in all—coming, somewhat, back under control. All told, I think Ellie and I broke up only three times.

MY NEXT GIRLFRIEND, Christina, is one of the people in this world I admire the most. She took every episode of my insensitivity toward her and, with great creativity, aimed it back at me. Christina has been the Roadrunner to my Wile E. Coyote. I left Christina, after a year and a half, with brutal swiftness, when I met and fell in love with an actress who seemed poised to have some success as a film star. Shortly after our breakup, Chris requested a meeting at my apartment. She told me she hated me, and that she wished me pain and hardship for the rest of my time on earth. "You're a monster," she said. "I hate you, and I wish you a miserable life." At the time she said it I thought her tirades were proof that I'd made the right choice. Of course, it wouldn't have been so hard to hear if I hadn't been afraid it was true.

A year after that I was left even more suddenly than I'd left Christina when my film star girlfriend was seduced away by the lead singer from a rock-and-roll band we'd discovered and enjoyed together. I'd encouraged her to use her publicist to secure us seats to one of their sold-out New York shows. After a great night at the concert, having shared post-show beers with the band, we got home and heard a message from the band's manager inviting my girlfriend, and only my girlfriend, to return the next night. The next night came and my girlfriend, exercising some short-term decorum, didn't go. But within another week she was gone for good. I recently spent a couple of evenings with her for the first time in more than five years and asked if she was still in touch with her rock star pal. "Yeah, he calls once in a while," she said. "But it got too crazy for me. I was always hearing about some nineteen-year-old or another."

What did she expect? I thought. Trace the story back just half an inch, and you could ask the same of me.

Christina, whom I'd left for the actress, wrote a brilliant play in the aftermath of our breakup, which contained at least a few references to her rage toward me. It changed her life, gave her a pride and professional identity she'd never had before. I fell in love with her for the first time, including the year and a half we'd been together. I began an extended series of approaches in which I begged her to forgive me and take me back. I think there were a couple of occasions when she came close, but, ultimately, the most she ever offered was one of the parts in her play. I therefore got to be close to her by spending five ferociously hot summer weeks living in an unair-conditioned college dormitory in the decrepit town of Poughkeepsie, New York, where I performed in her play nightly and watched her flirt with and, at least in my imagination, be seduced by a varying string of men around me. Christina and I never so much as kissed again. I admire her as much as anyone I've ever known, at least partly because she allowed me to break up with her only once.

One brief affair that stands out in my memory from the years since was with a woman named Melissa. Ordinarily, this wouldn't have been an involvement that would have required an official breakup. We dated only briefly, and started to when she'd barely ended a long-term relationship with a man she'd been living with. Their split was so recent that, in one of those gloomy New York stories, they still shared an apartment as roommates in Brooklyn. After our second or third date Melissa started referring to me as her "boyfriend." She couldn't understand why I went pale with each reference. When I told her that I felt there was a difference between dating, exploring compatibility, and being in a committed relationship, she started referring to me as her "bad boyfriend." I broke things off cleanly after only a few weeks. I thought I'd done it kindly. I told Melissa that I liked her quite a bit, that I thought she was a fantastic and loving woman, but that I just didn't think the kind of deep feelings I craved were going to develop. Melissa was taken aback. She complained she'd been misled and betrayed.

"What do you *meeeeaaaaaannnnn*?" she moaned in outrage. "How can you *saaaaaaaaay* that?" In one of the great exit lines I've had hurled my way, she demanded, "If you didn't love me, how could you take me to see Ricki Lee Jones???"

I really didn't know what to say.

And now I've split up with my second fiancée, Patricia. I thought for a while we'd get back together, but, so far, it's back to a one-for-one average. In looking back over my various relationships I can't help but feel sad. I wish I could go back and love the person better than I did the first time around. Some people claim to live lives free from regret. It sounds great, but I can't relate. Most of my memories are made up of just that, especially in regard to relationships, and most especially in regard to their endings. Each one can be defined not by whether I've felt regret about them but by how large or small those regrets are in comparison to all the others. I've lived under the illusion perpetrated upon us by our novels, motion pictures, and fairy tales: that there is a perfect partner out there waiting for us; that, once

found, our relationship will be free of conflict; and that the only fric-
tion between us will be the kind that culminates in orgasm, preferably
simultaneous. No matter what age I've reached or how many relationships I've saved or sabotaged, I've still got a long way to go when it
comes to just growing up. In regard to love, I feel both overdue and
unprepared. But in one of the most optimistic patterns of my pes-
simistic existence, when it comes to love—just like life itself—I still
can't wait to give it another shot.

My Life Story

I FIRST FELL IN LOVE with Patricia as a result of selling off my past. I suppose that's one way to get rid of it. Or to feel like you did.

In 1995, I optioned the motion picture rights to my first book, *Time on Fire*, to an old friend, Rick, who'd become a TV star and was looking for a film project to direct. Rick and I had met and become great pals more than ten years earlier while working together on an off-Broadway play. We'd bonded, as actors often do, out of mutual frustration over the direction rehearsals were taking. We started having beers to talk over the scenes, and found ourselves making more progress during our drunken laugh-fests than we did in the theater during our sanctioned work sessions. We were playing a pair of mind-altered teenage punk rockers, and the play took place in the men's room of the legendary New York music club CBGB. Late-night alcoholic investigations were probably the most appropriate form of research.

Our first steps into that hallowed—and beer-and-urine-drenched—

hall of rock and roll history demonstrated how drastically we'd need to alter ourselves to portray the inhabitants of the club. Rick was a clean-cut figure, muscled and robust. He looked like a well-reared kid from suburban Long Island. I had already cut my hair into a timid attempt at a Mohawk by leaving an Astroturf length of hair on either side of the longer middle stripe. That didn't stop me from looking like a well-reared kid from suburban Long Island, too. I just looked like a well-reared kid who'd gotten himself a funny haircut.

The other people in the club were the real deal. I'd never witnessed such mass emaciation outside documentaries about droughts and genocides. Spikes and razor-sharp ridges of shellacked hair extended up to thirty-six inches above the heads they sprouted from. Rick and I dodged whenever anyone around us passed or turned, afraid of being sliced apart by hairdos that could have cut concrete. We laughed at our own timidity, then stifled the laughter out of fear of being filleted: there were knives strapped to the legs of a significant percentage of the clientele.

Rick and I had a great time in the play. Neither of us was well known in New York, and we wanted to make our marks. But our nightly shenanigans were mostly geared toward making each other laugh. There was a woven metal garbage receptacle on the set filled with all kinds of junk. We'd rummage through it as part of the action of the play and take turns coming up with business that might make the other crack up. Rick took to dousing himself with the remnants of a can of soda during a euphoric outburst. One night I found a red felt-tipped marker deep in the bin. I started drawing diagrams of the webs of veins running under the skin up and down my arms.

After our run Rick and I spoke or saw each other just about every day. We were in our early twenties with few responsibilities to anyone other than ourselves, and were always on the lookout for girls to flirt with. Our skills in attracting them far outpaced our success in bedding them. We'd tell each other the most torrid details of our dates, and share the most tortured details of our fledgling relationships. Once one of us had an established girlfriend, we were usually so tormented over the loss of all other possibilities that we'd betray the one we'd worked so hard to win. These caddish qualities weren't restricted to us, or the men we knew. The young women we were with often instigated their own versions of hit-and-run collisions, with only minor variations.

Just like all our friends, we then hurried off to confess our sins to our psychotherapists as if they were priests. Since we all got our therapeutic recommendations from one another, this small assortment of mental heath professionals was hearing about the emotional pummelings we were giving one another from every angle. It wasn't unusual for boyfriends and girlfriends to see the same therapist. If those shrinks weren't constrained by professional restrictions, theirs would be the books I'd want to read.

Rick and I also developed just a hint of a big brother/little brother dynamic to our relationship. I'd been working as a professional actor for several years longer than he had, and had already appeared in at least a couple of Broadway productions. I'd made films. I'd worked with movie stars. It wasn't unusual for him to call and ask for advice about agents, about which job to accept, or even about which woman to date.

"Hey, Ev. I met this girl last night . . ." phone calls would often begin.

". . . so what do you think I should do?" was a common end to whatever story was told.

Rick and I were both supportive of and competitive with each other. We'd see each other's performances, and meet each other's prospective partners. The plays or films we performed in were often the same ones the other had auditioned for, and the women we dated were often the same women we'd seen date other friends. For the most part, these conflicts were easily managed. We enjoyed the work we were doing, we enjoyed watching each other do it, and we had great appreciation for the individuality we each brought to it. We were play-ing hard and working playfully, all while operating in a comfortable zone of small-time success, gaining reputations that were still below the national radar.

THESE FUN AND GAMES were all interrupted when I developed leukemia and had a series of hospitalizations from which few believed I'd emerge. Rick was among a group of friends who visited during my extended out-of-town hospitalizations. They dropped what they were doing and traveled two hundred miles to spend several hours with an extremely ill and possibly doomed companion. That's no small ges-ture. For all the festive decorations one might find in a hospital's bone marrow transplant unit, it's not a cheerful vacation destination. And I was not always a gracious host.

"Hey, Ev. How's it going?" my arriving friends might ask.

"How do you think?" was a standard response.

Rick and our pals took out hotel rooms in Baltimore, where I was undergoing a bone marrow transplant procedure, and made a party out of their trip. They arrived in my hospital room the second morn-ing bleary-eyed, telling tales of having raided the hotel kitchen's refrigerator during a marijuana-fueled frenzy the night before. A security guard had arrived, and they'd had to hide for hours in cabi-nets under the sink.

These visits always stirred up a mélange of emotions for me. I was deeply moved that they'd made the effort to see me; I would have been wounded if they hadn't. Still, it was agonizing to hear of the adven-tures I was locked away from. It was hard to connect to the laughter over their exploits the night before when I'd spent the same evening vomiting into a plastic basin. They took my girlfriend out for much-needed dinners and nights out on the town, respites that probably extended her patience with my situation. I was appreciative to the point of tears. At the same time, I often imagined that they took turns sleeping with her behind my back.

Toward the tail end of my medical trials my friendship with Rick was knocked off course when he was cast in a network television show that became a hit. He relocated to the West Coast for some years while filming episodes, and was cast in several choice roles in feature films. I was jealous of his success, and couldn't help but wonder whether a similar elevation in status might have awaited me had the illness not kept me imprisoned for the better part of four years.

I was also uncomfortable with the reversal of our big brother/little brother roles, with him now being the more experienced business-man after his contentious negotiations with his television network. Rick had attained a level of operations many of us only dreamed of, with high-powered agents, lawyers, business managers, and publi-cists all on his payroll. With his popularity from his television show continuing to rise, he certainly wasn't seeking me out anymore for advice about girls. They turned to stare wherever he walked. Our friendship continued once I was well, but we were never as close as we were in more innocent days.

SINCE RICK HAD been among those to witness some of my suffering firsthand, it made a certain amount of sense that he thought of my book when he went looking for material for a film. Rick wasn't the first to express interest. Others had already approached. I'd once ten-tatively agreed to option the material to a producer associated with Tri-Star Pictures. The producer, a friend of my literary agent, approached days before I gave the first public reading of the seeds that would eventually grow into the off-Broadway production of my one-man show. The offer he made on behalf of the studio came with the caveat that it was only good up until the play's premiere. Once the production opened to the public, when competitors might see it, Tri-Star's offer would be off the table. Being the novice I was, I took my agent's advice and accepted the deal, which was never negotiated to completion.

The Tri-Star deal fell apart over the film studio's contractual "template," from which it would not deviate. The template stipulates that every property purchased by the studio must come with sequel and prequel rights to all the events and characters contained within. They—whoever "they" are—gave no weight to the notion that what was being pursued was autobiographical. They could not understand that I was not in a position to grant them perpetual rights to the life stories of every person I'd written about. Nor was I interested in granting them automatic ownership of everything I ever wrote, or simply did, for the rest of my own life. Not that Tri-Star's retreat was tragic. The morning after a review of the play appeared in *The New York Times* I got a call at the theater inquiring about the rights from a director by the name of Mike Nichols. Mr. Nichols beat his own hasty retreat when my literary agent convinced me that I was obligated to honor the still-uncompleted (and soon-to-be-defunct) deal we'd theoretically agreed to with her friend the Tri-Star producer.

The predictable update to this story is that, though these approaches were all made well over a decade ago, no film has yet been made from the material.

IT WAS NEVER MY DREAM, upon uttering the words that made up my version of my life story, to have them duplicated (or, more in tune with most screenplay adaptations, distorted) on film. But I'd discovered the power of the tale. While performing the stage version, or traveling upon the book's publication, people of every stripe—including, but not limited to, patients, relatives of patients, and health care workers—came to hear the story and sought me out afterward to talk. The experience inside the theater was a communal roller-coaster ride. Audience members found themselves laughing at the horror, then becoming horrified by what they were laughing at. They choked up with tears, then forgot and laughed all over again. If I was going to make a movie out of the material, I wanted to stick with the storytelling instincts that had succeeded onstage and on the page.

Most of the exploratory conversations Rick and I had focused on procedure, rather than the story and how it would be told. We talked about what our working relationship and responsibilities would be. We fantasized about inviting people we'd idolized to work with us. We were two great friends who'd dreamed of such an experience for years before it had any chance of becoming a reality. Rick's success made it seem as if the adventure would actually happen. The project seemed to have the potential to be both a thrilling creative experience and a rekindling of a friendship between two men who'd done a lot of their growing up together.

There were only a few occasions when we engaged in more detailed explorations of the actual work at hand. Since Rick was consistently complimentary about the book and its insights, saying things like, "I can't wait to see how you transfer the sperm bank scene to the script," it seemed implied that our working relationship would begin with my writing a screenplay that I'd then present to him. I expected, based on our conversations, that we'd be like-minded in our views. Still, I expressed concerns about the film veering too far from the principles that drove me to write the story in the first place.

"Why would I want to make a movie that wasn't true to you and your vision, Evan?" he asked. "You're the best resource I'm ever going to have."

Even more time was spent enduring excruciating periods of legal haggling to work out a deal. I was trying to get written confirmation of most of the promises Rick had made to me in conversation. I'd insisted, and he'd promised, that I be the sole screenwriter on the project. I wanted protection from being replaced. I wanted the right to be present on the set, and even the right—though rare for a screen-writer—to have approval over casting choices. Rick's lawyers offered stiff resistance to these clauses, even though they were guarantees he had offered up in person. The creative meetings between the two of us were still filled with his pumped-up hyperbole. These discussions contrasted drastically with his demeanor on the occasions I tried to cut through a negotiation impasse by appealing to him directly. Those phone calls were handled with spectacular detachment, and always culminated in his claim that he wasn't aware of any of the contractual details.

"I just leave those things to the lawyers," he'd say.

I always pictured him, when he made those statements, wearing earphones and sitting in front of a bank of video monitors, overseeing every utterance in regard to his business interests. But I've got no proof.

Rick's talent agency was also eager to conclude the deal. At the time he was courting me he was represented on several fronts—as actor, director, and producer—by the William Morris Agency. William Morris was also the employer of the lone literary agent representing me, who encouraged me to accept the ill-fated Tri-Star offer and to shoo away Mike Nichols. The president of William Morris was a man named Arnold Rifkin, who was said to have a "Zen garden" incorporated into his lush office at the firm's headquarters in Beverly Hills. While I was performing the stage version of *Time on Fire* in Los Angeles, in the midst of one of many stalled moments of our negotiations, my William Morris agent informed me that her boss, Mr. Rifkin, wanted me to come in for a meeting. It's not every day the president of the most famous talent agency in the world requests my presence, so the invitation stirred some excitement.

As my meeting with Arnold Rifkin approached, my mind was filled with fantasies of how he might influence my career. Would he offer me representation as an actor by William Morris? Might he choose to take me under his own wing? I might as well have been skipping along the Yellow Brick Road, so unrealistic were my expectations—and so Oz-like did The Mighty Rifkin turn out to be.

I was nervous about my appearance before the wizard. There was, indeed, some form of rock garden and fountain arrangement that I passed on my way to his inner sanctum. Once I'd seated myself across from him, it wasn't long before it became clear that Mr. Rifkin's mission that day was simply to secure something his client wanted, and that I was the obstacle standing in the way of his client's desires. The fact that what his client wanted was the right to tell the story of my catastrophic illness and unlikely recovery—as told and popularized thus far by myself—didn't seem to weigh on anyone's mind but my own.

I don't mean to suggest that Arnold Rifkin was rude. He was polite and asked about my play. He expressed admiration for my history. He seemed impressed by my determination in telling my story. He exuded something I would place on a map somewhere south of sincerity but well north of brusqueness. And then he made a proposal so ludicrous I found myself wondering whether I'd be serving myself better by pretending to take it seriously, or by laughing out loud. In a tone resembling a dentist who offers a good child a lollipop, Arnold Rifkin told me that the William Morris Agency also represented the Busch Gardens family theme park. Should I consent to option the material to his client, I was told, he'd look into the possibility of creating a ride there based on the material in my play. About my leukemia. And how badly I'd suffered from it.

What is he talking about? I thought to myself. Can he possibly be serious? Can he think I'm going to be swayed in my choice by his dangling of the possibility of a "Time on Fire" ride at Busch Gardens? What would it be called? "Patients of the Caribbean"?

My response was to nod weakly. It's a habit of mine I'm unhappy with to this day: my tendency to accept being treated as someone less intelligent than I am, in order not to insult the person who's insulting me.

WHEN MY FRIEND Rick grew exasperated with the length of time it was taking to conclude a deal, he made a pronouncement over the phone.

"I want you involved every step of the way, Evan. I want you involved in casting, and I want you on the set every day. I want your input on every decision, and I'll never make a movie you wouldn't agree with. It'll be like a codirectorship, in everything but title."

Anyone who's got his wits about him, when encountering a phrase like "a codirectorship, in everything but title," might respond, "Why 'in everything but title'? If you want input in the capacity of a co-director, why not back it up with the title and make it mean what it says?"

But I didn't ask those questions. I swallowed hard and said, "Okay."

I didn't keep my mouth shut entirely. Before I agreed to terms, I made it clear I'd go into business together only with his promise that (a) I'd get to write the script I wanted to write, (b) I'd have a hands-on, explicitly acknowledged (though still ill-defined and eternally undocumented) role as a cocontributor, and (c) I'd have the assurance that the final film would be a faithful representation of my own thoughts and beliefs in regard to its subject matter. How I expected either (b) or (c) to be enforced is still a mystery to me. Apparently I was doing what I'd been encouraged to do much of my life by people who knew my doubting nature: I was running on faith.

Over the next few months Rick included me as a crucial element of the sales pitches he was making for the film. I was (I like to think) impressive and charming when brought in to meet the executives of the company that eventually came through and offered financing for the film. I was thrilled when we got the go-ahead from them for him to direct his first feature film and for me to write my first commissioned screenplay.

I was, however, taken aback when Rick invited me to spend part of the summer working on the script with him at a property he'd rented in Southampton. It wasn't the invitation that startled me, but his instructions. Rick followed his description of the sumptuous estate we'd be sharing with the dictum *"I do not want you to write a word before we start working together."*

I'd already been working on a script for some time. I'd started to fool around with various structures and ideas as soon as we started shopping the project around. Then, when I was officially hired by the financing company as the screenwriter, I was told to keep in touch with the vice president of the company, to show him my drafts, and to hand him my finished script when the delivery date arrived. They'd hired me in a separate deal, under a different contract, from the one in which I'd optioned the property to Rick. They'd also reimbursed him for that expense, effectively taking over the option from him. They were my employers now. It hadn't occurred to me that my friend was going to want to closely supervise or, worse yet, participate in the entire process of writing the script. I'd assumed I'd write a draft, and then there'd be rewriting in the form of notes and adjustments from both him and the producers to cater the script to the tastes and inclinations of each. Like a couple who'd managed to throw a terrific wedding without learning any of the communication skills needed for a good marriage, we were ready to fly off on our perfect honeymoon.

A FEW YEARS earlier Rick had shared with me some of the lifestyle changes his success had ushered in. Most of the changes were matters of practicality, like having a personal assistant take care of chores and return phone calls. Others had seemed a touch odd. The simple trick of returning his phone calls from various corners of the world, of trying to call at appropriate hours after figuring in time zone differences, was complicated by the instructions he left to ask for him under various assumed names. "Dick Trundle" is one I remember. "Scott Snead" another. There were occasions when I was told I could remember the name he was using by spelling his real name backwards.

I knew his TV show was popular, but were people really trying to track him down around the globe? This isn't Oprah Winfrey we're talking about. It isn't Paul McCartney or Michael Jackson. Hell, it's not even Ted Danson.

Then there was the issue of the assumed names themselves. "I'm registered as Reggie Jackson," I heard once on my answering machine.

What's up with that? I thought. Didn't using the names of people much more famous than he was offset the intended benefit, whatever that benefit was supposed to be? Or was he actually trying to *increase* his profile by convincing people he was there, but that he was someone other than who he was? I was confused.

The personal assistant, on the other hand, was an adjustment that impressed me. This, I have learned, is one of the key tools utilized by successful people. "I don't do anything for myself anymore," Rick told me. "I don't pay my bills, I don't do my laundry, I don't go to the supermarket."

"How does your assistant know what to get?" I asked.

"She knows what I like."

What about the good old impulse purchase? I wondered. If someone else did all my shopping, I'd end up eating the same thing, at the same time, every day of every week. I'd go mad. Apparently a reluctance to delegate personal chores is one of the facets of my personality that's stood in the way of my enjoying greater success. It's possible Rick didn't know what he wanted on any particular day, either. Maybe his personal assistant was like TiVo. The more she was exposed to his preferences, the more accurate became her future predictions. A nifty feature.

By relieving himself of the duties most people have to slog through before even beginning their day's work, he'd freed himself up to be able to concentrate on whatever he chose. He used his time to read and educate himself in regard to filmmaking principles and theories. Of course, few things are more tedious, or perhaps even dangerous, than a person who's come to view himself as an expert solely from theoretical readings. But I put my misgivings aside, since the Hamptons were a nice place to be during the summer. Plus, I learned his assistant was to be briefed about my own culinary preferences.

"What do you like to have for breakfast?" I was asked. "I'll have Kristin fill the refrigerator in the guesthouse for you."

MY FIRST DRAFT of the screenplay was a bloated overweight mess. It came in at 175 pages. For those of you not familiar with modern screenplays, that's somewhere between fifty-five and eighty pages too long. Still, I wasn't concerned. There were portions I was immensely proud of, and the length was, at least in part, in acquiescence to Rick's doctrine of doing no work before we sat down together. I felt that arriving with what was clearly a rough first draft would go as far as necessary toward reassuring him that the script was very much a work in progress. I expected he'd be able to see that there was plenty of room for shaping it together, and that there would be abundant opportunities for him to put as much of an imprint on it as he might feel necessary.

Our first day of work together consisted of my old friend Rick reading my 175-page screenplay to me out loud. Himself. Playing all the parts. Badly. I was flabbergasted. Besides being flabbergasted, I was appalled. It's not that one individual reading a screenplay a cappella is unheard-of. I'd witnessed such readings in writers' groups. I'd also read about it being done by renowned filmmakers with recalcitrant screenwriters in a few books. The same books, apparently, my friend Rick had been reading in preparation for our work together. What disturbed me was the presumption that he had gained a level of expertise qualifying him to play the role of teacher to my student. Rick's awkward recitation was followed by his setting the script aside, pulling out a set of three-by-five-inch index cards—a common screenwriting tool used in the first steps of designing a screenplay from scratch that I'd used and dispensed with weeks earlier—and announcing that we were now going to begin all over again. Together. Page one. Go.

Really. Just like that. Rick wanted to preapprove, not only what scenes were going to be written and in which order they'd occur, but every single word that would be said within them. He also wanted to predetermine the precise length each scene would run, *down to an eighth of a page*, before a single word of dialogue was written. Before writing a single word of Scene One, he wanted me to declare the precise length I'd give to Scene Seventy-six. I tried to find a way to play along and make it work, but my patience ran out within a matter of minutes.

"Look," I said. "I can't tell you how long each scene is going to be before I start to write any of them. That's not going to work." I told him I wasn't comfortable writing as a team, or even writing in his presence. I told him that I understood the structural requirements of a screenplay, and understood how to outline one. I even added that I was happy to outline the script, in a more general way, with him. But the precise details of each scene would depend on what inspired me as I wrote, and what proved to work best as I progressed. I pointed out that the length of scenes and the pace of the final script could be shaped and sculpted in the rewriting process, allowing for the freedom I depended on to create . . . well, *creatively*.

"I'm not prepared—in fact, I won't be *able*—to write my own adaptation, of my own book, of my own life story, under your supervision, to your word-for-word specifications. That's not what I signed on for. That's not what we agreed to."

This was the first half of day one. The second half consisted of my being scolded—complete with reddened face and bulging jugular—for having "deliberately disobeyed" him by writing a draft of the script on my own. I received a recitation of elementary principles of screenwriting from books and lectures I'd read and attended myself. I also heard, for the first time, the doctrine he intended to govern our work from that point forward. Growing more and more agitated, he told me that, whatever I wrote, the film that ultimately resulted would be his film, no one else's film, and while he'd certainly take my feelings and opinions into consideration (thank you very much), he alone would choose what went into it, and how every moment would be rendered. Regardless of whatever assurances had been made, it became clear that—in spite of the lovely surroundings and Kristin's superintuitive expertise in amply supplying my favorite fruits, nuts, and cereals—I was in deep trouble.

From there things got worse. Every morning, out came the index cards.

"Scene Twenty-seven, the hospital hallway. How many pages?"

"I don't know."

"Give me a number."

"How can I give you a number, Rick? I haven't written it yet. None of it's been written. None of it's likely to come in at the length we've assigned so far."

And then the screaming would start again.

"You can't write without a blueprint!" I was told, as if I didn't know this already.

"Writing a script is the same as building a house: you need a foundation!" Which is true.

"When you're in the paradigm, you can't see the paradigm!" (From Syd Field's book *Screenplay.*)

"Every movie is about one idea!" (From Robert McKee's "Story Structure" seminar.)

"The rhythm and tempo have to accelerate as the act climax approaches!" (Robert McKee, again.)

Those are my attributions. Rick spoke as if these insights were his own. I'm not arguing against any of them. I simply wasn't happy having them shouted at me by someone no more qualified than myself. (I would like to point out that even Mr. McKee states that "any of these rules can be broken, if something more important is put in its place." I know, because it's in my notebook from when I attended his seminar. Underlined. Twice.)

By now Rick would be leaning inches from my face, enraged, rabidly screaming.

"You're being deliberately uncooperative! I'm the captain of this ship!" (*Mutiny on the Bounty,* I guess, Charles Laughton, 1935.)

"There's going to be one captain, and it's going to be me!" (Cap'n Crunch, 1972?)

Faced with his tantrums, I usually tried to summon the calmest demeanor I could.

"Listen," I'd say softly. "You're going to have to stop screaming at me. I understand that you're the one who's going to direct the movie. But I'm going to write it. And I'm not going to write it, word by word, here under your watchful eyes."

"So you're refusing. You're refusing to work with me."

"No. I'm saying I'd like you to tell me what scenes you want from the book. Tell me what scenes you want that aren't in the book. I'll write them. Then you can give me notes. I'll rewrite, incorporating the notes as best I can, and we'll work from there."

"I can't have you writing without me. That's a waste of time. If you write by yourself, you'll just write things that don't work for me, and we'll be right back where we started."

Then he simply took up where he'd left off, as if we'd never had any conflict at all. "Two pages. You'll do the hallway in two pages. Now give me some shorter scenes. We've had a couple of long scenes, so now I'm going to need some shorter ones."

He was smoking a cigar as he barked these orders. My old friend Rick, with whom I'd shared so many laughs over so many silly moments. With whom I'd created my own history, and whom I'd helped create his. Many people had criticized him to me in more recent years. They saw me huddled with him at a party and came over to talk after he was gone.

"Do you know him?" they asked. "He's so arrogant."

My old friend Rick, whom I defended on those occasions—strenuously—had come to fancy himself the auteur of my autobiography. As the result of a few seasons on a TV show, a couple of roles in feature films, and a few books he'd read, Rick had come to see himself as the reincarnation of Orson Welles. As they say in show business, "Oy, vey."

I FELT ATTACKED, misled, and trapped. I had already accepted money and agreed to terms. I was under obligation to deliver a screenplay. And I was heartbroken. One moment I seethed with rage over the seventeenth of Rick's daily slew of insults. The next moment I realized that this was what it looked like to watch a friendship die.

Of even greater concern than friendship and professional obligation, however, was that I had only one life story to tell. I wanted to make sure it wasn't told in the dismal fashion of most of the films in its genre. More than that, I wanted to make sure it didn't fall into the genre most people would have categorized it as belonging to. The fact is there has *still* never been an American theatrical release film in which the main character's life-threatening illness drives the plot, and in which the character survives. It's never been done. Never, ever. They always die. Every single time. Conquering this issue was one of the creative challenges that had me excited about the prospect of writing the script. I wanted to give the film an unconventional, uncertain ending. I wanted to leave the audience with an image of the lead character physically safe, but walking off into an unknown future. This goal, too, turned into a point of contention.

"You can't break the rules until you've mastered the rules," I was told. (To my amazement, a quote from my sixth-grade gym teacher upon doing a reverse, double-pump layup instead of a traditional one during basketball drills.)

I sensed that the showdown wasn't destined to go my way, and that ultimately I was going to have no say whatsoever in how the film got made. Besides my emotional investment in the material being battled over, I didn't know how to deal with being badgered, bullied, and shouted down for hours on end. In one of the oddest ironies of my strange existence, I had somehow mastered surviving treacherous ordeals while not knowing very well how to take care of myself in a creative collaboration.

At night, after "working hours" were through, I was living in my old-friend-and-current-adversary's guesthouse. I didn't own a car. I was 150 miles from my apartment in Manhattan. Unless I was willing to walk out on the whole endeavor, I had nowhere to go. I'd slink back to my quarters and wait to get up the next day to go at it all over again. I'll leave it to others to decide whether it's a distortion or not, but I felt like I was fighting for my life all over again. Or at least fighting for the right to tell the story of it in a way that made sense to me.

AND THAT'S WHEN Patricia stepped in. She became my knight in shining armor. More accurately, she became my knight in a ten-year-old, beat-up, rusted-out Volvo she called "the Moo Monster." Patricia was playful and childlike in that way. She named her cars. She even spoke to them.

"Come on, girl," Patricia would appeal when the car made ominous sounds. She'd pat the dashboard as a gesture of encouragement. I know she did these things with at least a bit of a sense of humor about them. But I think she also believed her relationship to the car had a positive effect on its performance.

Patricia heard the pain and strain in my voice while I was working on Long Island. She got in the car and traveled to me on a work night to be by my side. And that's where she stayed.

Patricia and I had been dating for only about six months so far. Her rescue mission in the Moo Monster was the first time I witnessed her ferocious way of expressing her loyalty, and I found it deeply restorative. Hers wasn't an "I will stand up for him because he is right" call to arms. Her stance was, "My man is being attacked, and I will defend him. My man is being attacked, and his enemy is now my enemy, *and will be from this day forward.*" Patricia would hear none of my layered interpretations of Rick's behavior, or confessions of my own culpability. "He's a monster," she declared. "He's treating you like shit, and I hate him for it." And she did. It was as simple as that. And I felt loved so deliriously as a result that it moved me to fall in love with her.

Patricia's exhibition also caused me to question whether I'd ever lived the meaning of the verb "to love." It's easy to *feel* love for another, I recognized. But I also learned that *to* love someone is a much more active, and generous, endeavor than anything I'd undertaken before (let's hear it for the slow learner at the back of the room). The fact that it was also an exhibition of the precise differences in our characters that would eventually doom us was an irony that wouldn't become clear for some time.

Patricia continued to visit during my luxurious servitude. Things grew ever more tense between Rick and me, and less and less was accomplished. I finally shortened the length of my stay from three weeks to ten days and arrived home eager to get to work on my own. I gained strength from Patricia's support. She worked as a creative executive for a major film company. Anyone who's familiar with creative executives in the film industry knows the title doesn't necessarily mean they possess any great insights—or even any creativity. But I respected Patricia's opinion. She complimented the work I'd been doing and it meant a great deal to me.

I also drew courage and inspiration from conversations with screenwriting friends more experienced than I. Over the next few weeks I completed what I thought was a lean, clever draft of an appropriate length, handed it to Rick, and awaited his response. He seemed to have accepted that I was going to write the screenplay of my choosing, while allowing him to have merely a great deal of influence, as opposed to absolute authority.

My liaison to the production company throughout these struggles was a man named Bob. Bob had proven himself to be perceptive in terms of script and story, and canny in his ability to compare versions. He had often asked how things were going in my work with Rick, and I'd always insisted things were fine. Eventually, as he continued to probe, I decided to share with him some of the trouble I was having. Now that Rick and I had moved past some of our earlier difficulties, we were having disagreements over which version of the screenplay to turn in. I also shared with Bob my dilemma in regard to whom to hand the damned thing over *to*. Along with his refusal to agree on an acceptable version, Rick had insisted that I not hand the script over to my employer, as they'd instructed me. His command was that I deliver the script to *him*, allowing him to hand deliver it to the production company.

I could understand Rick's desire to be perceived as the mastermind of his project. But he was putting me in an impossible (not to mention humiliating) position. I had my own contractual obligations.

Then there was the issue of trust. I wasn't sure, at this point, that my old "friend" would deliver to the company the same version of the script I instructed him to.

Bob seemed sympathetic to my plight. He suggested that I allow Rick the honor of making our official submission, and that I should hand over to Rick the version of the script I felt best about. But he also invited me to simultaneously prepare for him another version, one that might offer a good representation of what I felt Rick was pressing me to write. Bob wanted to read both and decide for himself which was superior. This would mean twice as much work for me, but the opportunity for an opinion from a keen third eye made it seem worth the effort.

Once Bob had read the scripts he discussed with me his impressions of the two versions. He agreed that mine had more humor and emotional complexity. He also agreed it would make a better movie. The problem was, it didn't appear my version was the movie Rick intended to make. Bob told me that Rick had delivered the script I'd put my name on, but he'd also arrived at their offices with another stack of index cards. He'd sat with the president of the company, with Bob, and with their director of development and had pitched his own scene-by-scene reworking of the material as his preferred option. Bob was regretful. But he said there was little they could do to force Rick's hand. Their agreement with him was to finance a film over which he'd have complete creative control.

I was impressed with the deal Rick's team had cut for him. No rides at Busch Gardens for my old friend.

"I'm afraid there's nothing we can do about it," Bob said. "We've got a deal with him."

"Well, I don't."

"Yes, you do," said Bob. "Or, at least you've got a deal with *us*. He optioned the material from you, and then we bought the option from him. As part of his deal, we gave him a guarantee to direct. So when we bought the rights from you, that ties us all to him. There's no way this company can produce the film without using him as the director."

"What if I didn't have a deal with you?" I asked.

"But you do."

"What if I didn't?"

"You *have* a deal with us. That's what we *paid* you for. When you signed that deal, you signed over all the underlying rights to the book and the story."

There was a pause.

"You signed the papers, right?"

It wasn't asked with any kind of alarm, or even inquisitiveness. It was asked the way you ask a question you think you already know the answer to, in order to prove a point.

AMID THE STRUGGLES with Rick, I'd taken the agreement that granted the production company the rights to my life story and slipped it into a drawer. Unsigned. It wasn't done in a scheming manner. It was a matter of practicality.

The contract we'd agreed to distinguished between two fees I would be paid: one was for writing services. The other fee would be compensation for the underlying rights to the story. Separate amounts had been negotiated for each. The only money I'd received so far had been accompanied by a letter stating, "Advance payment for writing services." It made no mention of any part of the payment being for the purchase of the underlying rights to the story. I cashed the check for writing services, and went to work writing a script. I figured the remaining amount of my fee was being withheld until I provided an acceptable one.

I wasn't concerned about the bulk of the money that was still due. I could understand the company's desire to hold off on paying for the rights to a story I hadn't yet proven I could write to its satisfaction. By that same reasoning, I didn't see why I should sign a contract granting the production company those rights before it had compensated me for them. So the papers remained unsigned. Only after it became clear that the promises and assurances Rick had made to me weren't going to be honored did I knowingly decide to let the contract ripen and ferment. It turned out to be a choice that would, for the ninth or tenth time (if you include the literal as well as figurative senses), save my life. Or at least the story of it.

"You signed the papers, right?" Bob asked.

The face I made wasn't a smirk, and it wasn't a grimace. It was more like a shrug. A shrug that said, "I'm not saying I did, and I'm not saying I didn't." I had no idea why I was being so coy, or any idea, really, of anything I was doing. I changed tactics immediately.

"No," I said. "I didn't. They're sitting inside a drawer in my desk."

It was one of those glorious moments in life. Not glorious because of their content, but glorious because of their purity. Glorious because of the irreversibility of the action. Like the moment you tell a woman you love her for the first time. Or the opposite, that you've been having doubts about the relationship. When you confess an affair. Or like when you tell someone that they don't actually own the rights to your life story. That they don't have the right to produce a movie on the subject in whatever way they choose, regardless of how you feel about it. Glorious, because no matter what you suddenly feel about the decision you've made, there is no turning back.

As for Bob and his reaction, it was impressive. It was clear that his mind was working along several tracks simultaneously. He appeared startled. He seemed concerned that he and the company were in deep shit. He looked as though he needed to have a talk with his boss as quickly as possible. But he also seemed to be scanning his mind for the new possibilities that might be raised by this revelation. He began to ask me about those possibilities immediately.

"So who *would* you want to have direct the picture?"

We talked about all sorts of individuals, from the impossible, to the improbable, to the realistic. Within minutes Bob offered his own opinion.

"What would probably make the most sense would be for *you* to direct the movie."

Of course it's something I'd thought of. When you spend weeks, or months, working with someone you think is mucking things up, it's hard not to think, "Oh, man, *I* could do this—and better, too." But it wasn't something that had entered my mind until the problems with Rick became unmanageable. Even then, I'd had no thoughts of it being a possibility. I could hardly believe Bob had brought it up. That made it even harder to accept when, once the unsigned contract became known throughout the company, I was accused of having planned such a mutiny all along.

RICK HAD PAID me $15,000 for the option on the material a year earlier. The production company had reimbursed him for that expense when they took the option over six months later. At that time they'd paid me $20,000 for the "advance on writing services." That $35,000 was what I'd been living on for the past year. I offered to give back every cent I'd been paid, even though it was already nearly gone. The company's response was to initiate a series of legal maneuvers to defend their right to tell my life story, with my permission or without it. I was forced to hire a well-known film industry lawyer who, upon hearing my predicament, eyed me with barely concealed scorn.

"You're the first person who's ever asked me to defend his right to give money *back*."

Finally I decided to appeal, once more, to Rick. Surely, I thought, my old friend would be able to understand a direct, human approach, concentrating on the morality of the situation, instead of the business aspects. I apologized for whatever mistakes I'd made along the way. I asked him to understand that I'd lost faith in our ability to make a film that would make the statements about my existence that were important to me.

"Forget about contractual issues," I said. "Do you think it would be right to make a movie about the things I went through, knowing that I don't agree with the way you're representing them, and knowing that I don't want it to happen?"

Rick said, "They're telling me they want me to direct this movie, Evan. As long as they tell me that, I'm obligated to stay involved."

"But, Rick," I said. "They can't make the movie without my signing over the rights. And I'm not going to do that as long as you're attached. I'm sorry. But it's not going to happen."

"Well," Rick said, "I guess we'll each have to play out our hands, and see who rakes in the chips."

SEVERAL MONTHS LATER, after dozens of threats of lawsuits were hurled my way, a note arrived at my lawyer's office. It was an acceptance of my initial offer to repay the production company the money I'd received in exchange for its dropping all claims. The letter arrived on a Wednesday, and stated a deadline of the end of business on Friday. I had less than forty-eight hours to come up with $35,000. I had $7,000 in the bank.

First, I borrowed $12,000 from my parents. Then I arranged for a $20,000 bank loan to be issued within twenty-four hours—no small trick for someone with my level of assets. I combined it with every penny of my bank balance, as I had to pay back the money with interest, and had a check delivered to the production company's office by

Friday afternoon. Shortly thereafter my lawyer received a letter relinquishing all claims. A few signatures erased one nasty little dispute of little consequence to the world beyond our small circle.

JUST AS POWERFULLY as the telling of the story drew people toward me, the selling of the story fragmented relationships. My old friend who'd wanted to direct, the people at the production company, the lawyer who handled the undoing of the deal. The first film company to have approached, Mike Nichols, and the agent who'd recommended I turn him away. As inclusive and nurturing and nutritious as I'd found the act of telling others the story of where I'd been, I found an equal level of divisiveness and depletion in the act of trying to sell it off, or get it back from those who believed it was theirs. It was a costly miscalculation. But worse was the loss of a friend from bygone days.

Meanwhile, Patricia, a woman who struggled with her own substantial difficulties in sharing with me the most personal details of her own life, became the staunch defender of my right to control the disbursement of the details of mine. We hunkered down together through the legal threats. Patricia encouraged me to protect the story as both the asset it was, and for the value it held for me and for those it had touched. She reminded me of the hundreds of letters I'd received from people thanking me for telling what they felt was their own story, and the thousands more who might have felt the same way and not made contact.

"So many people have been inspired by you," Patricia said. "People who took strength from your recovery. Who wouldn't have been able to put their own feelings into words. And there'll be more like them every day who'll be looking for their own inspiration. That's an incredible thing. You can't let anyone take that away and ruin it."

Patricia is a wonderful woman. We were, for a time, not only a functional couple but also deeply in love. The juxtaposition of one old friend working hard to betray me while a new love was working to defend and support me made Patricia's actions feel all the more impressive.

WHAT I WAS left with after everything was resolved was my history. The tale of where I've been. Sharing my history was an act that has had tremendous impact—for me, and for many who've let me know what it's meant to them. For now, my life story is back where it belongs: in my possession.

Or, actually that's not true. My life story is back where it belongs: in possession of me.

My Clock Ticks, Too

MY CHILDREN DON'T live with me. I learned recently, through articles in the newspaper, that their place of residence had been ordered closed by the New York State Department of Health. I immediately made some calls and, concerned for their safety, made arrangements to have them transferred. Today I left my apartment to pick up my children and take them to their new home.

On my way to the Empire State Building, where my kids have been stored for close to ten years, I thought the same thoughts as many neglectful fathers.

"If something is going to happen to my children, I'm going to be with them when it does."

My children don't really exist. All that exists is the potential for their existence, and even that is in desperately short supply. Since I was successfully treated for (and ultimately cured of) leukemia, I've been sterile. As a precaution against just such a probability, I had semen stored years ago, to be used to attempt a pregnancy sometime in the future. At the time, when I was twenty-four years old and unsure of even short-term survival, the fact that inseminations using frozen sperm had resulted in full-term pregnancies after up to ten years of cryopreservation (the deep freeze) offered me all the breathing room I could've ever imagined needing. I was in a love-filled, committed relationship. Our future together, in which parenthood would feature prominently, was one of the most compelling reasons to walk the hellish treatment path that promised the only hope for any future at all.

Traveling the subway toward my imagined offspring, I thought back on my young life. I'd rushed into the excitement of an acting career at the age of seventeen, reveling in the travel and adventures while my friends were settling in for four-year stints at state universities. After the five-year battle to save my life, I scoffed at the notion of stability while attending the weddings of those same friends. Their children were born, and I felt my pose of superiority substantiated by their jealousy over my latest in a string of lovers. The rest of them are filing cooperatively along the line that runs safely down the middle of the road, I thought. I'm filling my memory banks with a priceless treasure trove of experiences to look back on someday.

STARING INTO THE steam pouring out of the gurgling tank of liquid nitrogen where my emissions had spent ten years, I thought back on the women I'd loved. I'd had a seventeen-year stretch of serial (more or less) monogamy, with an assortment of beautiful, intelligent, and talented women. They were women who, for the most part, had their own agendas for the future. Agendas that had more to do with fulfillment achieved through career accomplishment than through building a lasting connection with another human being. The medical technician showed me the thin plastic straws wherein my forsaken extrusions were suspended in an airless, unconscious existence. He plunged them into the portable metal tank in which I would carry them across town. The liquid nitrogen hissed and boiled as it swallowed them, and I wanted to say, "I'm sorry, kids. I fucked up. I failed you. I can see where I went wrong, but there's not a lot I can do about it now." Like any father who's put himself first for too long, I wanted to beg my children's forgiveness, to circumvent their anger and limit the damage done. But those are not my children. Not yet. Only a part of myself, spat out long ago, the denial of which has damaged no one as much as me.

"You wanna watch them transfer your specimens, right?" asked the receptionist at my children's new home. Apparently this is a parental tradition of which I'd been unaware. Not wanting to miss out on any more milestones, I bore witness as another technician, in another lab, immersed them again in their unfathomably frigid womb. There, they'll continue to wait.

"So, for how long can you use this stuff?" I asked the man who was planting my seeds in the tank. "How long does it stay good for?"

"We've had successful pregnancies with sperm that've been cryopreserved for up to thirteen years," he said.

So there's still time for me. Time to get to know those children I might never meet. I left through the same unmarked door I came in through. I hit the street and reentered the swirl of humanity in the same way I reentered my life. Saddened by what I'd seen of myself. Determined to make the next phase of life more meaningful than the last. And eager to meet the woman who'll help me bring those kids to life.

Tiffany '99, Sotheby's '01

I N THE SPRING OF 1999, I spent $5,000 on an engagement ring. It seems a paltry sum, in retrospect, for a symbol of everlasting commitment and devotion. But my thoughts about it at the time were mixed. I was happy that my fiancée, Patricia, was repulsed by more ostentatious—and costly—jewelry. I was simultaneously amazed to witness the transformation of this formerly utilitarian, status-abhorring, non-makeup-wearing woman into a wide-eyed, diamond-crazed consumer. I don't care how grotesque a generalization it is—and it *is* one—but something happens to the vast majority of otherwise left-of-center American women when confronted with the iconography of a diamond engagement ring. When confronted with the dueling sentimental and consumerist realities of their force-fed-since-birth fantasy: The Wedding.

After more than a half-dozen trips together to Tiffany, interspersed with stops on Forty-seventh Street to seek out bargains, I finally became disgusted with myself for contributing to the dilution of what should have been a romantic gift. So one day, while Patricia was at work, I went to Tiffany alone, screwed up my courage, and purchased the ring that had given her the biggest smile—but with slightly larger stones. It was a platinum band, styled with the classic Tiffany taper, accented by gold settings, which held a single diamond, bordered on either side by slightly smaller rubies. A very classic engagement ring. Quite beautiful. From Tiffany. The ring was placed into a black velvet, spring-loaded presentation case. The case was then placed into the iconic powder blue Tiffany gift box, which was nestled amid tissue paper in an identically colored Tiffany bag. I paid the bill with a credit card, took my tiny package, and was out on the street.

"Never pay retail," echoed in my head. I knew a similar ring could have been created for less than half the price. But that process, in our two trips to Forty-seventh Street, had seemed tawdry. It involved sketches and planning, handling crude lumps of metal that were yet to be transformed into delicate bands, and selecting gems from scattered splotches of stones that made them seem the cheap pebbles they actually are.

On the street outside Tiffany I headed for the bus. A single finger supported the braided string from which dangled the bag holding my $5,000 cargo. A bag too small to hold a sandwich. The wind could have blown it away. I've never been frugal with money. I enjoy having it, whenever I do, and enjoy the items and experiences it can purchase. As generous as I've been toward others, and myself, I've rarely plunked down $5,000 on any single item with one swipe of a pen. I was feeling giddy about the surprise awaiting Patricia that evening, imagining her delight and even experiencing some myself. I was overjoyed to have finally stuck with a relationship long enough to get even close to marriage. And I was feeling nauseated by the size of the expenditure.

"It's the cost of doing business," I told myself.

I didn't mean it coldly. It's a line I've found useful in my professional life. If you want to play in the big leagues, you've got to invest the way others are willing to. Travel the coasts, wear decent clothes to your meetings. This is the woman you want to spend your life with. You want to make her happy, and this is a gesture. This is, after all, the beginning of your marriage. It's the price you pay to be in the game.

In October of 2001, I traveled across town to Sotheby's to sell the ring. It had been sitting in the back of a drawer for more than a year, since it had been returned to me. Another gesture. I'd hung on to the ring just as I'd hung on to the idea that the relationship could be rescued. When rescue failed, I continued to cling to the ring and some small semblance of hope, but this time for resuscitation. When it became clear there'd be neither, I decided to offer a gesture to myself. I called Sotheby's and scheduled an appointment to have the ring appraised and listed for auction.

It's an embarrassing call to make. It involves explaining to a number of strangers, as you're handed from department to department, that you've got a barely used engagement ring to sell. It involves describing the ring over the phone, and admitting that for your $5,000 you purchased a diamond of less than half a carat, and two rubies that combined weigh barely more than that. It involves pulling that same pale blue gift box out of a drawer, opening it, and peering inside that black velvet case. It involves wrestling with the memory of the gift, and the joy it once gave you. It involves remembering the odd thrill I got from kissing her ring finger, of holding it in my mouth while we made love.

At Sotheby's, an officiously polite blond woman several years younger than I joined me in a small cubicle and sat down behind a desk. On her left hand was a diamond several times larger than the one I had come to sell. I'd glanced through the auction catalogues scattered on the desk while waiting for her and seen spectacular jewelry, including diamond engagement rings, with prices ranging from $30,000 to $6.5 million. I was hoping to get twenty-five hundred.

"Please place the sale item on the tray," the woman said, extending a plastic tablet toward me. After noting that I was listing my item along with a ring case and a Tiffany gift box, she left the room to have the stones examined and appraised.

As impressed as my unassuming fiancée had been with my decision to graduate to larger stones, the Sotheby's executives were equally underwhelmed. They were all pleasant, in their decidedly impersonal way. Their behavior was how I would expect funeral home employees to comport themselves. Professional. Discreet. But never for a moment are they going to join you in your grief.

The appraisers estimated the sale value of the ring at between $2,500 and $3,000, and I was persuaded to list it with a reserve—or minimum price—of $2,000. Sotheby's would take twenty percent of my revenues, as well as twenty percent from the purchaser. This meant that should the ring sell for its minimum (as it eventually did), I would receive $1,600 for the $5,000 ring. Sotheby's would rake in eight. Only back out on the street did I think about eBay.

It was a cold day, still not even noon, and I was already exhausted. I felt despondent and on the verge of tears. Emotions piled up in layers, each one complicating the one underneath. It's awful to break up. And it's awful to deal with the dirty business of dissolving financial entanglements. The fact that a substantial loss of money came into play was painful, but even more painful was the realization that, in the face of the emotional loss, I still gave a shit about the money at all. But I did.

"The price of doing business," I told myself again. "That's what it costs to get out of the game."

I WANTED TO call Patricia. I wanted to share the pain with someone, to announce that the ring had been sold. Who would be better able to appreciate the horror than she? But I reminded myself that that wasn't appropriate. She'd suffered her own black hell in returning the ring to me in the first place. In hunting for an apartment in the worst real estate market anywhere, ever, and moving out of the home we'd shared. This was my mess to clean up. I fingered the cell phone in my pocket, itching to dial someone. And then I realized where I was.

I'd been wandering south in a daze from Sotheby's, at Seventy-second Street and York Avenue. I looked up to see that I was standing across the street from the hospital I'd almost died in, several times, many years before. It had been more than thirteen years since I'd set foot inside that building. Almost exactly sixteen years since the first time in, and more than thirteen since the last time out. I'd thought many times about stopping in, whenever I passed close by on foot, or in a bus or taxi, heading up First Avenue past Sixty-eighth Street. But I'd always decided not to make the turn and travel east. This was the first time I had the entrance in sight. The first time in more than thirteen years I'd ventured this close.

I tried to rouse myself from the swamp of despair that was beginning to envelop me. I seized on the glimpse of the hospital as a means to remind myself how far I'd traveled since those awful days. No matter how painful my current emotional state was, I was lucky to be alive and experiencing it. I found myself crossing the street toward the doorway, just to have a peek. Just to see if what I remembered was true. I thought about the ring I'd left behind at Sotheby's, the break I'd made with the past, in that regard, and I wondered if today would be the day I went back to visit a more distant portion of it. I got to the main entrance of Memorial Sloan-Kettering Cancer Center, where the stunned, the stupefied, and the devastated got in and out of taxis, and I walked in through the door.

My reluctance to return to Sloan-Kettering for almost a decade and a half wasn't simply a matter of emotional fragility and bad memories, though they played their parts. My experiences there had been horrifying, and my life, in my opinion, had been endangered by disease and indifference in equal measure. Still, my decision to steer clear of the building for so long had little to do with my feelings toward the hospital and its employees. It stemmed from my expectation of ill will on their parts toward *me.*

I hadn't simply retreated from Sloan-Kettering years before, happy to have recovered and regained my life and liberty. I'd written an off-Broadway play and a book about my experiences, in which I excoriated the institution and many of the individuals who worked there. I outlined the methods I'd developed for circumventing debilitating hospital rules and procedures. While promoting the book I was interviewed by newspapers, on radio, and on television—local and national—over the course of two separate ten-city book tours. I used every opportunity to malign an institution I'd come to see as corrupt in its complacency, and abusive—sadistic even—toward its captive customers. If that wasn't enough, I'd spent a good portion of five or six years performing my brand-name-specific show for groups of medical professionals at conferences and symposiums in Boston, Orlando, Houston, New York, Las Vegas, Chicago, Los Angeles, San Francisco, and Washington, D.C. The last time I did the show was at an event that kicked off a difficult post-engagement vacation for my fiancée and me. It was May of 1999, and we flew to Europe, where I was slated to give the keynote address at the international meeting of the Institute for Healthcare Improvement in Stockholm, Sweden. I told my tale gleefully, seducing world-renowned physicians and administrators into laughing at my portraits of their boorish colleagues. I relished the revenge I was able to exact upon the institution I felt had pushed me around. My fiancée was in the audience that day, twirling the Tiffany ring on her finger. I wasn't concerned about upsetting *myself* that day at Sloan-Kettering. I was afraid of being recognized by an irate employee who might try to knock my head off.

I had to lie to gain admittance for my return. Security measures were in place, because of the September 11 terrorist attacks, and only patients, family members, and other authorized visitors were allowed up the escalator and into the reception area.

"I'm here to visit a patient," I told the uniformed guard, who directed me up to the information desk. I rode the escalator, passed the desk without speaking, and walked into the heart of the lobby. The room, as seems to always be the case years later, was smaller than I remembered. The gift shop was at one end, with cushioned chairs spreading out from it, facing picture windows overlooking the sidewalk.

Those chairs were a special destination fifteen years before. They were reserved for the privileged, those who were well enough to travel off the hospital floor and gain a closer glimpse of the outside world, perhaps never to be experienced again. I'd sat there with friends I'd grown up with, with friends from drama school and beyond. Me, hairless, hooked up to an IV pole, and, at 111 pounds, twenty pounds thinner than at high school graduation eight years earlier. I spouted optimistic slogans at my freaked-out companions, who searched my gaunt face for the terror behind my proselytizing eyes. More than twenty years ago now. I'm not in touch with any of them anymore.

I scanned the room, studying the faces and postures of the people huddled about. It was a busy place. But the ingredient I was searching for—the pain—wasn't readily apparent. A few were clearly patients, dressed in robes and attached by tubing to IV poles, but fear wasn't shrieking off them like I'd have expected. I saw a couple dozen people dressed in street clothes collapsed in chairs, presumably visitors, packages piled at their feet. They weren't crying, though; no one was being consoled. They seemed just like anyone else in Manhattan: tired and stressed, perhaps, but doing their best to make it through another day.

I wondered how much time I'd spent living in that building. Between six and eight months was my guess, spread out over the course of two or three years. Thank God I got sick before insurance companies instituted the "managed care" nightmare. I chose where I thought I'd be best treated based on information I gathered, as best I could decipher it. I made some mistakes along the way, but far fewer than would have been made on my behalf by a company looking to cut corners.

That residency time estimate doesn't include the dozens of full days spent as an outpatient, in waiting rooms and examination rooms, or strapped into gargantuan, groaning machinery. Those six or eight months were the ones I spent with my clothes hung up in the closet. With trinkets and false comforts on the side table next to my hospital bed, failing miserably at creating some semblance of home.

I HAD THE URGE to explore. The cafeteria was the hospital's melting pot, where nurses, physicians, patients, technicians, family members, and administrators all mingled. I knew it was only a few steps from the end of the lobby opposite the gift shop, but I was afraid to go. Even standing in the lobby, the easiest place in the eighteen-story structure to remain anonymous, I felt conspicuous. I don't know why I feared discovery so much. I hadn't been seen or heard from by any of the people I'd insulted for nearly a decade and a half. Unless they went to the movies or watched television. Or read newspapers, or listened to the radio. Or leafed through magazines, or browsed through bookstores. Or attended medical conferences, or . . . well, you get the idea. Though from my memory, few of those people actually *did* any of those things. What I remember of the oncologists at that hospital was the single most isolated, non-pop-culture consuming group I'd ever come across. I remember one of my first doctors there, a man named Leonard Zweig—a monstrous, sadistic schlub, as I recalled—telling me about the marvels of the brand-new technology of compact discs, *years* after most people's vinyl collections had cracked, mildewed, and crusted over. He shared his discovery with me as he screwed a large needle into the back of my hipbone to extract bone marrow. I had no idea if any of the people I'd been treated by fifteen years earlier still even worked at the joint. There's a high burnout rate in a field where eighty percent of your patients die from the disease you're attempting to treat.

I decided what I needed for my reconnaissance mission was an ally. There was a woman I'd befriended during my years as a patient at Sloan-Kettering, a nurse I'd stayed in touch with for some years afterward. Her name was Olivia, and she was every bit the full-fledged incarnation of compassion and dedication you'd want from someone in whose hands you were to place your care. Years after my medical treatments ended I'd call Olivia on the phone to give her updates on my life. I'd listen in amazement to her tales from the battlefield, wondering how she could still be operating within the same theater. I'd invite Olivia to join me and my friend Jackie, who had been my girlfriend during the years of illness, for dinner, or Olivia would take us to a Mets game, to sit in her uncle's seats right behind home plate. Olivia was one kernel of proof that I wasn't the ingrate many of the doctors and nurses had experienced me as being. If I could befriend and enjoy her, I reasoned, it must demonstrate that I'm capable of appreciating those who truly were dedicated to delivering compassionate medical care. I went to the staff phone to see if I could have her paged. If for nothing else, just to prove that she really did exist.

"OH . . . MY . . . GOD . . . !" Olivia said into the phone. "Oh . . . my . . . God . . . ! Don't move. I'm coming right down."

Olivia is an ebullient woman. She talks fast, gets excited, laughs easily, and while her instincts lead her toward relentless optimism, she has no trouble handling sarcasm or doling out a dose of her own. Olivia had come to see my off-Broadway show, and she'd read the book it was expanded into when it was published. She was able to integrate her passion for her work with her agreement with many of my criticisms of the place where she did it.

Olivia had aged noticeably since the last time I'd seen her. Her body had thickened, and her hair was beginning to gray. Still, I recognized her immediately. We hugged and giggled, a rare display of euphoria within those walls. When I told her I was nervous about running into some of the doctors I'd taken to task in years past, Olivia dismissed my concerns.

"Oh, they don't even know you insulted them," she insisted. "Are you kidding? Their egos are so huge, they wouldn't even be able to tell."

I told Olivia about how difficult the year had been, and about the morning I'd spent across the street. I told her how, in the aftermath of my most recent relationship, not to mention the international catastrophe just a few weeks past, I'd been thinking about volunteering as some sort of patient advocate or advisor at a hospital somewhere. I was finally interested in finding a way to be helpful to somebody other than myself.

"That is so *great!*" Olivia said. "Why don't you do it here?"

That would be an odd twist, I thought.

"I'm not sure that's the best idea," I told her. "I don't imagine I'd be welcomed with open arms."

"Don't be ridiculous," Olivia insisted. "They'd be happy to have you. Look," she said, pointing down the hall just past the information desk. "That's the volunteer office right there. I'm going to walk you over."

I knew I'd have a lot to offer. The fact that I'd suffered so much difficulty in my own treatment gave me a useful perspective from which to help others who might be struggling themselves. Olivia ushered me past the information desk I'd avoided on my way in. I felt a chill as I passed the demarcation line between the public areas and the interior of the hospital. We said our good-byes, promised to get together soon, and I opened the door to the volunteer office and walked in.

.   .   .

THINGS WOULDN'T PROVE as simple as I'd hoped. There were forms to fill out, and an official interview process to endure. Apparently, I was going to have some explaining to do.

Complete disclosure: that was going to be my policy. Whoever I need to speak with will hear straight from me that I'd had problems with the place when I was a patient. I'd tell them that I'd spoken freely in the years since I'd been an inmate, and that—as much as such a thing was possible—I simply had the desire to be helpful, on an interpersonal level, with others who might be suffering through similar circumstances.

A woman introduced herself to me as Jane Rockingham-Dystal, the coordinator of patient volunteers. She told me we'd need to set up an appointment for an official interview on another day, but she asked me to join her in her small office for an informal chat. I gave her a brief overview of my history, including the details of my book. I assured her I no longer held any ill will toward the hospital or any of its employees, and I shared with her my belief that, especially in light of the way I went through my illness, I could be a valuable resource to patients.

Ms. Rockingham-Dystal listened intently, and she seemed intrigued by my story. She said she looked forward to hearing about the experiences I'd had as a patient—good and bad—as well as the work I'd done as a health care writer and activist. She concurred that, as an actor and a figure visible in the media, I had an unusual platform from which to offer opinions. Perhaps, she offered, I might even be welcomed by patients who might otherwise be resistant to assistance. She told me about the volunteer program, what important work it was, and how central it was to the success of the hospital. We set up an appointment for Friday of that week, and I left the office with my head spinning. It was the most pleasant, welcoming encounter I'd ever had in that hospital.

. . .

THE MOST COMMON question I've been asked about my illness and treatment over the years has been "Do you think things at Sloan-Kettering have changed since you were a patient?"

My response has always been that I can only guess. "I assume things must have changed, somewhat," I say. "But I have no way of knowing."

After all, the world has changed so much since then. Awareness of the need for compassionate medical care has increased. The benefits of proactive patient involvement—already proven by the time I was a patient—have become even more widely embraced. It would stand to reason that some of those principles have taken hold, even if I'd personally found them lacking during my own treatment.

After my visit in the volunteers' office, I wondered if I'd just experienced my first taste of some of those changes. I crept down the narrow hall that led from the lobby toward the cafeteria. I turned the corner to face the entrance to that bustling room. There, I came up against the question of whether things had ever been the way I'd perceived them to begin with.

The room was teeming with white lab coats and blue surgical scrubs. If I were to run into any of the people I'd known years before, this would be the place for it to happen. A parade of medical professionals swarmed around me. I had a brief premonition and swung to my left. The first being to come into focus looked vaguely familiar. As soon as I glanced at the name tag pinned to his lab coat, I pulled back around the corner to hide. My heart was pounding. I leaned slowly toward the edge of the wall to take another peek.

"Leonard Zweig, M.D.," the tag read, the word "Attending" stitched into the fabric.

Holy shit, I thought. There he is. The man I'd represented as the most malevolent creature in the story of my survival. I'm staring at him, maybe ten feet away. I wonder if I should go up and say hello.

I vetoed the idea quickly and settled in to observe. What I saw from my perch bore no relation to what I remembered. He seemed a small, nebbishy man. Benign. Where I remembered someone portly and unkempt, this man was trim and well groomed. I remembered a man who was a loner, disliked by even his colleagues. This man was laughing easily with a large group. Maybe he's changed, I thought. Maybe he's happier now. But even the age was incompatible. The Leonard Zweig I was spying on toward the end of 2001 looked younger than I remembered the evil Dr. Zweig being in 1985. I'd guess the age of the man I was watching to have been in his late forties, maybe fifty. But that meant the doctor I remembered, the one who'd scolded my father for phoning him at home to ask if it was all right to give me a Valium the night of my diagnosis with acute leukemia, would have been no more than thirty-five. That was six years younger than I was, as I cowered behind the corner studying him. Could he have been that young a man? Could my memory have so distorted him? If so, what other personalities, characteristics, and events might I have twisted over the years?

My rage years before hadn't been unfounded. Of that I'm certain. But maybe, just maybe, it had been misdirected. The indignity of illness is the severest one I've ever known. When it was exacerbated by understaffing, lack of supplies, arcane and archaic traditions, not to mention occasional lapses in judgment and carelessness on the parts of medical professionals—all while battling a devastating disease—it became too much for me to bear silently. Now, after loitering in the lobby and examining the staff in the cafeteria, I couldn't locate the evil intent I'd assigned to them back when I'd been in their charge. More than anything, the place had the feel of a tiny, inbred community, like a small, provincial high school. Obsessed with itself, perhaps, but there are worse crimes than being oblivious to the world beyond one's neighborhood. Tunnel vision in the quest of a cure for cancer can't be any worse than tunnel vision in the search for a successful sitcom, right? Had I been mistaken in my condemnations? Or is there something in the dynamic of desperate need and excessive authority that can't be discerned by those not enmeshed in the equation? Had I misinterpreted people struggling to do their best under impossible conditions? Or did they all now seem so innocuous simply because I was no longer subject to their sway?

I walked out of the hospital into a perfect, cool, autumn afternoon. I had such a feeling of rebirth and of hope for the future. Of hope, if this makes any sense, that I might have been mistaken about my past. I thought maybe some good might come out of the car wreck of a day. Maybe, by falling as low as I had, I could now make a positive impact, which might make up for the carnage I'd wrought the past year. I wandered along side streets and up avenues. I lost track of my route and stiffened from the cold as evening enveloped me walking across Central Park. I let myself into my apartment and hit the button on the answering machine.

"Hello, Evan. This is Jane Rockingham-Dystal at Memorial Hospital. I'm afraid I won't be able to interview you on Friday. Thank you. Good-bye."

It was spoken in a bright and optimistic tone. One that suggested a scheduling conflict, as if I should call to find a better day. But she hadn't said that.

"I'm afraid I won't be able to interview you on Friday."

Not that she won't be able to interview me *at all.* Not that it's been decided another interview will be *unnecessary.* Yet, there were no instructions to call back and reschedule.

" . . . won't . . . be . . . able . . . to . . ."

What . . . does . . . that . . . mean . . . ?

I called several times over the next few days after conferring with various friends. Opinions seemed split over what to expect, or if it had been madness on my part to anticipate ever being accepted. Jane Rockingham-Dystal proved difficult to get on the phone. I would have thought she was avoiding me, except for the fact that I wasn't identifying myself before being told that she was unavailable. Finally, after more than a week had passed since the date of our canceled appointment, I sent an e-mail. I explained my confusion in regard to her phone message, especially when viewed in tandem with the cheerful tone of our meeting. I acknowledged, again, my awareness of the delicacy resulting from my criticisms of the hospital. I reiterated my belief that my experiences made me a more valuable resource for those now in the thick of things. I found myself getting worked up and emotional. I *wanted* to volunteer. And not just anywhere. I wanted to be a volunteer at *Memorial Sloan-Kettering Cancer Center.* I'd become enamored of the symmetry and didn't want to have it denied. About ten seconds after I hit "Send," my phone rang.

"Hello, Evan. This is Jane Rockingham-Dystal calling you from Memorial Hospital."

I was frightened to be on the phone with her. I had the feeling I knew what was coming and was concerned about whether I'd be able to handle it graciously.

"Evan, I would have told you this personally if I'd gotten you on the phone the other day," she continued. "I'm sorry if there was confusion about it. But after you left my office I spoke with the patient advocate's office. It seems there was a good deal of controversy regarding the treatment you received here, and in light of that, the feeling was it wouldn't be appropriate to have you working here as a volunteer."

My God, I thought. I'm like the bogeyman to them. I didn't know what to say. It wasn't a surprising reaction, yet I was shocked. First, that thirteen years after my last treatments there my name still carried so much weight that I could be nixed as a volunteer candidate within moments of vacating the premises. I tried to imagine how those conversations had gone. Had research been necessary? Did someone do a Google search? Or did the mere utterance of my name elicit a gasp?

And I was angry. In one moment I went from being eager to join their team, to wanting to blast them in the press all over again. How small-minded, I thought. Nothing's changed at all. It's the same story: you're either with us or against us. If you've got anything critical to say, no matter how constructive it might ultimately prove to be, we'd rather not speak with you. We'll banish you, ensuring nothing can ever upset our entrenched ways.

Even as I was shocked and angry, I was taken aback by my own naïveté. "What did you expect?" I asked myself. "You kicked the shit out of them, as often and as loudly as you could. Why on earth would they want to have you around?"

"Well, yeah," I answered myself back. "But I have something to offer. I possess knowledge and insight that could be helpful to them."

"Hey, Evan, you idiot," I heard myself shouting in my head. "They don't want it from you. Not now. Not anymore. Maybe if you hadn't set it up so accepting you would equal total surrender."

"Yeah, but . . ." I kind of whimpered to no one in particular. "That was a long time ago. It was all a long time ago. I'm over it. Why aren't they? I've forgiven me. How come they won't?"

And it took that long, but that's when the day achieved its theme. Because it was the same story with Patricia and the ring. It's why I still had the ring to sell over a year after we'd split, and why the year of try-ing to put things back together had failed. As I'd dragged myself and my self-pity to Sotheby's, and as I'd tried to soothe it by seeking the acceptance of those I'd traded blows with throughout and beyond my illness and recovery, I was trying to prove the impossible. That history doesn't exist if you'd prefer it was erased. That words haven't been spoken if you say you want them back. That love can be reoffered—and reaccepted—where it once was withdrawn.

"I've forgiven me. How come they won't?"

Maybe Sloan-Kettering would be a better place if the people there were able to listen to criticism without exiling the source of it. Maybe my ex would be a better woman if she'd been able to forgive the ways

I'd let her down. It's not for me to judge, especially considering my own participation in each of those equations. For me, the question is why I feel the need for their forgiveness. Why do I have such a strong urge to say, and do, exactly what I want under every set of circumstances, then to demonstrate that those words, and actions, don't have to have any of the consequences I don't want them to have? The mature act would be to accept a formula, and to alter one's behavior accordingly. It's called growing up, in most circles.

Only a child, or a madman, would attempt, repeatedly, to alter irrevocable laws. I've been acting the part of an insane Isaac Newton. I sit under a tree, where an apple falls on my head. Instead of recognizing gravity, and finding a different place to sit, I spend the rest of my days taping all the remaining apples to all the trees in the orchard, trying to prevent them from ever falling again. For a hard case it requires exhaustion to set in. Or, enough bruises—not to mention apples rotting above your head—to be willing to change. From now on, instead of looking back and trying to fix what's already happened, I'm going to carry forward the lessons I've learned. I'm going to try not to make the same mistakes again. Maybe someday I'll come upon an apple that's at eye level. I won't have to dodge it, and I won't feel compelled to keep it from falling. I'll just pick the apple off the tree, and take myself a bite. If I've learned anything from the past at all, I'll enjoy that apple. I'll savor it for the taste. Then I'll walk on by, leaving that particular tree behind.

The Two-Month Second Date

THE PROBLEM WITH falling in love with someone who lives 12,500 miles away is that it's hard to arrange for dates. In case you're not up on your geography, that's as far away from someone as you can get without leaving the planet Earth. It's only a fraction of the distance to the moon, but it's about thirty-five times farther than the International Space Station, to give some perspective. Despite the frequency of airline flights, if you live in New York City, Australia is very far away. Which means someone is going to have to travel.

In New York, uncountable relationships have been ruined simply as a result of partners living in different boroughs of the same city. For those who require spontaneity in their courtship rituals or hasty retreats after mating, even thirty-minute subway rides can spell doom. To get to Sydney, Australia, from New York City doesn't only take twenty hours of flying time on two different airplanes, it erases two days from your life due to crossing the International Date Line. Leave New York on Tuesday, arrive in Sydney on Thursday. As far as

Wednesday goes, don't plan any important meetings, because for you it doesn't exist.

Sane people (if you can call anyone dating someone who lives 12,500 miles away sane) might handle this by taking turns making brief visits. Insane people handle it by having two actors meet in Los Angeles, where neither party lives, to share an apartment for two months during Pilot Season, one of the most arcane and stressful rituals of show business.

For those not well versed in entertainment industry parlance, Pilot Season is the annual influx of actors into southern California for the three-month period when most new network television shows are cast and filmed. In many cases they are then recast and refilmed. Most of those shows are then shelved and never shown to the public. Amid this chaos lies hidden one of the many hushed-up facts of the entertainment industry: actors, much like grape pickers, are actually migrant workers. Our union's just a bit stronger than theirs. Or, wait. On second thought, it's not.

I spent the first two months of this new century in Sydney, Australia, making a television movie about the Three Stooges, playing frizzy-haired Larry Fine. I'd say I spent the winter there, but in Australia January means summer. The two months down under marked the eighth and ninth months out of the past eleven I'd spent working away from home, and away from my crumbling relationship. Abbey Leigh was an actress I met during my stay, a blond beauty brimming with all the bawdiness and snappy banter common to Australians. She was quick to smile, quick to joke, quick to poke fun at someone else, and quick to toss back a blistering retort should anyone be brave enough to poke fun at her. I was already down for the count with a crush when Abbey Leigh and I decided to spend Valentine's Day sunning ourselves in Sydney's botanical gardens.

It was a cold summer day in Sydney, and Abbey Leigh and I sat wrapped up under a blanket trying to stay warm. But not too warm. We spent hours that day gazing into each other's eyes, doing our best to keep our hands to ourselves. Every so often I got up and walked a polite distance to phone Patricia, my fiancée, back in New York to wish her a happy one-year anniversary of our engagement. (Note to all affianced individuals: If the engagement lasts a year and still no date is set, there *is* trouble in paradise.) I hung up the phone, then walked the several meters back to Abbey Leigh, wondering what on earth she could have been thinking during my absence.

Rolling around under a blanket was about as far as we took things during that stay in Sydney. Take that as my tepid nod to fidelity. I then spent the second anniversary of my marriage proposal to Patricia with Abbey Leigh as well—this time, at least, after Patricia and I had split up. Our second visit was in Los Angeles, where we'd decided to meet to "get to know each other." The only way to accomplish this was to be on the same continent. The only way to afford that was to live together.

Does that seem extreme? If so, think about this: If ever Abbey Leigh and I had decided that we wanted to date on a more extended basis, we'd have to have gotten married. Since neither was wealthy enough to forgo employment, and since neither could legally work in the other's country, we'd have been forced to wed in order to be in close enough proximity to date. For Abbey Leigh and me, our Los Angeles adventure seemed like a reasonable compromise. It seemed the sensible thing to do.

Nearly a year had passed since our initial meeting in Australia, and I'd continued to be plagued by thoughts of her. Living out my days in New York, coming up hard on forty years old, I'd take my daily (okay, my biweekly) jog around the reservoir in Central Park and obsess furiously over what I'd been obsessing over for months already. Every step, every heaving breath, every waking moment, every tormented hour of miserable half-sleep. Should I abandon everything I'd worked hard to construct—indeed, everything I'd worked hard to convince myself was right and good—or should I go ahead and marry Patricia?

My fiancée and I had come to love each other and depend on each other, but the fact was we hadn't been getting along. Or maybe that's exactly what we had been doing. What we hadn't been doing was thriving. We hadn't, on any deep level, been connecting, and we certainly hadn't been communicating. Open communication was what I craved, but it wasn't Patricia's style. When I met a beautiful Australian woman, seemingly mature for her years, whose quest in life was to communicate as emotionally as possible, and to connect as deeply and passionately as a body could withstand, I found her irresistible. I was thrilled to discover that her interest in me was equal to my admiration for her. What I wasn't proud of was that I'd met her while I was already engaged. On location. Shooting a film. Playing a Stooge.

I'd like to say that's as predictable as it gets, but I can't. Abbey Leigh was only twenty-five years old. That's not terribly original behavior for a thirty-nine-year-old man. But, I could point out, the full age difference was only in effect from January through August. Five months of the year the age difference was—numerically speaking—a mere thirteen years. Does that make it less tawdry?

I was drawn to Abbey Leigh as a result of her maturity and communication skills. This was in comparison to the woman I was with, who became paralyzed by any question more probing than "What would you like for dinner?" Then again, Patricia was a vegetarian who didn't like beans, rice, or very many vegetables. Her favorite meal was a bagel with cream cheese, in spite of the fact she was lactose intolerant. So even questions about dinner could be provocative.

But Abbey Leigh *was* too young for me. She eventually said so herself, during one of our later meetings after the relationship had been consummated. She just phrased it differently. She said *I* was too old for *her*. Only she used different words.

"You've got the lowest-hanging, droopiest balls I've ever seen," was how she put it.

. . .

ABBEY LEIGH WAS raised by her mother in Darwin, a humid port city near the equator on Australia's north shore. I've never visited Darwin, but it's been described to me as a place I wouldn't want to go. "Hardscrabble" was the word that was used, which made me think of a preponderance of bars, and the men stumbling out of them who'd want to beat me up. She'd been conceived when her mother, traveling through Central America as part of a dance troupe, crossed paths with an American soldier she knew only as "PJ, from Sarasota." A letter was sent via the U.S. military in an attempt to inform "PJ, from Sarasota" of the pregnancy, but no reply was ever received. Abbey Leigh was raised never knowing her father, whose identity remains a mystery.

This cocktail of facts had imbued Abbey Leigh with a striking combination of toughness and vulnerability. She was a volatile, titillating, ambitious woman-child, and her snappy repartee and skill at putting me on the defensive all contributed toward my infatuation. The fact that she had a deep fascination with human behavior and motivation, as well as a desire to understand her own actions and those of the people she interacted with, made her seem like an antidote to the limitations of the relationship I'd most recently been living with, or running from.

I was open with Abbey Leigh about my lack of availability even as I pursued her. Our attraction for each other was immediate, quickly became huge, and—aside from the fact that we kept it from being consummated during that initial stay in Australia—dominated our dealings with each other.

"You want to give me a massage?" Abbey Leigh once asked, amid her complaints of a muscle in spasm. "People use massages to relax. What are you trying to do, kill me?"

Or, in one of her more tender moments, as we were suffering toward our inevitable separation when I'd return home to New York, Abbey Leigh simultaneously complimented and criticized me.

"You're a gift," she said. "You're an Indian giver, but you're a gift."

Abbey Leigh was a clever girl. She also occasionally called me a coward. I never thought she was so clever then.

SHORTLY AFTER PATRICIA and I declared one of our intermittent splits, Abbey Leigh and I made arrangements for our reunion. We'd been corresponding via e-mail and talking on the telephone ever since I'd left Australia. At first she played the role of a good friend who understood and sympathized with the difficulties I was having. Then, as can often happen, the fact that she understood my frustrations better than my partner did made me feel closer to my confidante.

"You're beautiful," Abbey Leigh would tell me over the phone after I'd recounted one of my many shortcomings to her.

"I'm beautiful? What are you talking about?" I'd ask. "I just told you how selfish I am."

"Yes, but you feel bad about it. And you want to change. And you will."

It's hard to turn away from that kind of loving acceptance and encouragement. I ached for contact with Abbey Leigh while things with Patricia unraveled. An hour on the phone with her could transport me into a fantasy life in which I imagined feeling completely fulfilled. I'd hang up feeling as if I were emerging from a hot bath. I couldn't wait to see her again, this time without constraints.

The television show I'd been working on before my trip to Australia hadn't been renewed for another season, so I was eager to make this Pilot Season pay off by booking another show. This can be difficult to accomplish. Without going too much into the intricacies, television shows are cast under a system whereby actors, before participating in a final audition for studio and network executives, are required to sign away the exclusive rights to their services for a period of six years before they're even allowed to enter the room to compete for the job.

This protects the television networks from ever having to bid against one another for the services of an actor. I'm not aware of any other industry in which workers are forbidden from applying to more than one employer at a time, forbidden from attending an interview without first agreeing to terms (for six years!), and are then bound to accept the job should they be chosen, all before getting to meet their prospective boss. I'm fairly certain the practice is illegal, but that's a topic for another time.

Actors are also often not informed, prior to making those six-year commitments, in which city the television show will be filmed. That's right, just applying for the job often requires committing to a show whose location will be determined at a future date. The decision usually depends on where the production company can get the best tax incentives. Most often this means Canada. For the actor this means . . . well, leaving the country.

That's the type of offer I received while Abbey Leigh was flying over the Pacific toward Los Angeles. These deals are hammered out in the most frantic, last-minute fashion and have to be completed before the audition begins the next day. Negotiations often last deep into the night, continuing through the next morning and up to the moment the actor walks through the door to begin reciting his lines. Abbey Leigh walked off the airplane from Australia into a hailstorm of phone calls, low-ball offers, counteroffers, and my repeated declining of salaries beyond anything she'd earned in her life.

"I might have a job," I said to her as we walked out of the airline terminal.

"That's fantastic," she said.

Then, as we approached the car, which she'd have to learn to drive on the right, rather than the left, side of the road, I told her just how fantastic it was.

"It might shoot in Toronto."

Silence.

"Starting in four days."

Abbey Leigh stopped short of getting in the car.

"It would last about four weeks."

That was half the length of our scheduled visit, for which Abbey Leigh had traveled halfway around the world. I knew it was a horrible thing to greet her with, but the four weeks of work would pay wages on which I could live for a year.

"Don't worry, I won't go in for it if you don't want me to."

Things were starting to look up professionally. But for Abbey Leigh and me it was a less than auspicious beginning.

I WASN'T CHOSEN for the pilot, but that didn't mean Abbey Leigh wasn't made jealous in the following days by the number of appointments I had compared with her, or the salaries I was tentatively offered compared to what she was accustomed to getting paid at home. She was dealing, not only with the difficult emotions of sharing a home with someone whose career chronology was more advanced than hers, but also with the fact that she'd parked herself in a city—a nation—in which she was completely unknown. Abbey Leigh had already earned herself some respect as a film and theater actress in Australia. She'd given up a lot to come to Los Angeles.

None of those facts stopped me from being equally envious when Abbey Leigh was offered an Australian film from simply sending home a videotape she made at her L.A. agent's office. It had been a long time since I'd dated an actress, and I was starting to remember why actors congratulate one another when they date someone who doesn't work in the same industry. We tend to be less than gracious when it comes to our friends', or even our lovers', successes.

I'd also underestimated the challenges Abbey Leigh would encounter integrating herself into an unknown culture. Shopping (and driving, and even watching television) in a foreign country can require tremendous energy and intense concentration. I'd had a taste of it myself in Australia. Abbey Leigh often arrived home from running simple errands hours later than she expected, and wildly frustrated by her inability to function as proficiently as she was accustomed to.

Just a few days into our stay I woke from a nap to hear the front door slam. I followed the sounds of banging cabinets to the kitchen, where Abbey Leigh was unpacking groceries.

"What is it with you Americans? You can't keep the jam in the supermarket near the bread, where it belongs? It took me twenty minutes to find strawberry preserves."

I held up the jar. "Actually, there's a better brand than this."

"Don't get me started." Then she added, "I don't suppose there's any chance of finding Marmite?"

As tempting as it was to make fun of Marmite, I'd already learned that was a mistake to be avoided.

"Mmmm. Not much."

Abbey Leigh stormed out toward the porch, lighting a cigarette along the way.

"Could you please not smoke in the hou—"

"I'm not in the house, *lover* . . ."

Abbey Leigh liked to twist the endearment "lover" with the inflection one would use to sneer, *"Fucker!"* I learned this was intended to mean, "Get off my back."

You see? Even in code we understood each other. We were communicating.

". . . I'm on the terrace," she continued.

And by the time she'd finished the sentence, she was. But by then she'd already taken two drags on her cigarette, leaving clouds of smoke behind.

Yes, Abbey Leigh was a smoker. And I'm allergic to smoke. It causes instant irritation to my nose, throat, and lungs. Sometimes the symptoms from brief exposure are as simple as a series of sneezes.

Sometimes I'll get a sore throat, or cough and wheeze for hours on end. This is an illustration of one of the many differences between falling in love with someone illicitly, and living together successfully. For the former, there's no responsibility for the other person. It could even be argued the entire scenario requires disregard for the well-being of everyone involved. For the latter, there are levels of interdependence I was unprepared to live up to, or to acknowledge my own need for, until they were gone.

THE DIFFICULTIES DIDN'T all originate on Abbey Leigh's side. I'm no picnic to play house with, either. The selfishness that Abbey Leigh had commended me for feeling badly about some months earlier didn't magically disappear. I was consumed with the desire to find work for myself and wasn't as sympathetic to her struggles with Los Angeles as she would have liked, and that might have been appropriate. She was also understandably confused over my chronic sinus infections and the resulting medical terrors they stirred up for me. Abbey Leigh was aware of my past. But there's a big difference between knowing someone's story and living with that story's results.

"Do I feel hot to you?" I asked, every time I felt the slightest flush.

At first she put her hand to my head and told me, "No."

"What am I, your nurse?" she eventually started snapping back.

Abbey Leigh and I were getting to know each other all right. We were getting to know how little about each other we'd known to begin with. I learned that it's easy to be crazy about a person in counterpoint to another. It's a different trick to forge a relationship with that new person alone.

ON THE POSITIVE side (and there was one), Abbey Leigh enjoyed a sexual awakening in Los Angeles, and I got to enjoy a sexual reawakening of my own along with her. Many of the things we'd sensed about each other proved to be true, and our shared interest in open communication led to less inhibition, and more enjoyable exploration, than either of us had benefited from before. With Abbey Leigh there was none of the terror surrounding the exchange of sexual fantasies I'd experienced with some other lovers. It was a free-for-all. Talking with her was like playing "Can You Top This?"

I was also made dizzy with adoration by tiny glimpses of her. I passed the bathroom early in her stay and saw her sitting cross-legged on the blue and yellow tiles of the shower floor, the spray raining down around her. It was the way a little girl would arrange herself. I'd never seen an adult bathe that way. Abbey Leigh sat and examined and groomed her body for almost an hour at a time. Witnessing her pleasure and concentration was a revelation.

Abbey Leigh and I also both loved good food and restaurants. We loved to admire the dishes we'd create for each other when we cooked at home. I was particularly enamored of the Australian habit of complimenting a meal by calling it "beautiful," rather than "delicious," as if the taste of the food was merely one component of its splendor.

But the thrill I got from her naked innocence and her cooking didn't compensate for my annoyance when she cuddled up to me after smoking the one, two, or three cigarettes a day she'd already whittled herself down to on my behalf. I got irritable with her irritation when I asked, as a man of a certain age and with certain familial predispositions to heart disease, that she prepare more of the meals she cooked without butter.

The fact of whether or not you like living with a person depends on details as mundane as how long it takes them to get ready to leave the house, or how often they wash the dishes. But the most serious problem Abbey Leigh and I were having wasn't minor to me. It was an ingredient I'd never encountered in a relationship before. Whenever the two of us had any serious disagreements, or whenever we had minor ones, or really, whenever Abbey Leigh felt the urge, her way of releasing tension was to have a screaming fight.

Our fabulous sex sessions were often preceded, or followed, by Abbey Leigh throwing utensils around the kitchen. Without metric measuring tools she hadn't been able to accurately calculate a recipe and had therefore ruined a béchamel sauce—the cholesterol of which I could have lived (longer, perhaps) without anyway. She'd storm out of the house, sometimes several times a day, furious over something I'd said, in order to have a cigarette. She'd then storm out for another, muttering under her breath, after I wrinkled my nose over the tobacco smell that had infiltrated her hair since she'd gone out for her first. She sometimes shouted insults at me, insisting I scream back at her, for reasons I couldn't comprehend.

"What's the matter, Big Boy? Cat got your tongue?"

Big Boy? I thought. Cat got your tongue? What is this, a Barbara Stanwyck film?

"I feel like picking a fight," she'd say, smiling. There were times I was convinced she must be kidding. But there was nothing funny about her anger once she let it fly.

I TEND TO DISCUSS. I can see how for a certain percentage of people that might be frustrating. But I was unequipped for what Abbey Leigh craved, which was a brawl. In private, in our kitchen, or in public, in a quiet corner of a store, it didn't matter to her. Occasionally her wrath would erupt on a crowded street. I knew I was uncomfortable with the dynamic, but Abbey Leigh seemed perplexed by my reluctance to engage in battle. Then there were times when I lost my cool and screamed right back at her.

A series of auditions led to my being cast in a pilot created by two writers who'd worked on my last television show. Filming wasn't due to start for several weeks, so I essentially lived a life of leisure while Abbey Leigh continued to endure the indignities of casting calls in a city where she lacked the reputation she'd earned at home. The disparity in our situations only increased the tension between us. I hadn't realized how apparent the dynamic was to others until friends told me I'd been seen shouting back and forth with an Australian woman on Sunset Boulevard. I'm not claiming I never did anything worthy of her anger, but I wasn't used to the way Abbey Leigh expressed it. I knew it wasn't my style, and it wasn't the way I wanted to live.

THE FINAL FIGHT with Abbey Leigh happened outside a video store. I have no memory of what incited the incident. Maybe we disagreed on which film to rent. This time, afterward, she refused to get into the car with me to drive home. Instead, she lit a cigarette and stood defiantly several cars away in the parking lot.

"Get in the car, Abbey Leigh," I said.

She wouldn't turn toward me or acknowledge me.

"Get in the car!"

I wanted to get out and wrestle her into the automobile. I felt like I was a participant in a reality TV show I never would have even watched. We were only blocks from where we lived, so I simply drove away. I didn't go home, though. I parked on another street and sat alone in the dark. I became unbearably sad. I couldn't believe I'd reached another dead end. All the ingredients had changed, but the result was the same. Or all the ingredients had changed, except for me. I was the common link through all the fiascoes. From the very first kisses with my second-choice girl, through two broken engagements, to the absurd Australian-American odyssey.

I searched the car for the saddest CD I could find. Bruce Springsteen's *Tunnel of Love*. The album had been Patricia's favorite Springsteen recording. How ironic. The woman who couldn't reveal her own feelings was drawn to an artist's most nakedly confessional work. I remembered something Patricia had said to me on one of our last days together, as a rebuke of my rejection of her.

"You don't even know me."

She said it with contempt. I got the sense of someone whose depth I'd never experienced, which wasn't surprising. But her awareness of the dynamic was.

"Because you won't let me!" I'd wanted to scream. But it had been said already, in several different ways.

I sat alone in the car like a sullen seventeen-year-old. I listened in the dark as Springsteen sang about moving one step up and two steps back. It made me feel slightly better to know I was having similar problems to those Bruce had once had. Then I thought how his steps up had been so much larger than mine, or at least a good deal more profitable.

I thought again about Patricia, and I missed her terribly. Our relationship had been impossible, but, in retrospect, her withdrawals in the face of her fear seemed more appealing than Abbey Leigh's attacks. I wondered how I'd wound up with a stranger, and her strange ways, waiting for me at an unfamiliar, rented home, to share with me someone else's borrowed bed.

THE NEXT DAY Abbey Leigh broached the topic I was hoping she wouldn't. She wanted to know whether I'd been thinking about the future, and, if so, what my thoughts were. We were barely halfway through our scheduled eight-week L.A. stay, but I can't say she was jumping the gun any more than we'd already jumped it together. I told Abbey Leigh I couldn't see things continuing after our allotted time.

Abbey Leigh didn't yell or scream. She silently snatched her cigarettes from the pocket of her coat and went out to smoke on the terrace. She came back relatively calm, having wrestled with a decision I hadn't foreseen her considering.

"I won't be going home right away," Abbey Leigh announced. "I'd like to stay here with you, have as much great sex as possible, and then go home when I originally planned."

I quickly agreed. I was too frightened to upset her equilibrium. But, honestly, I wasn't terribly confident the two of us would be able to function better once we'd conceded defeat, as opposed to when we'd been filled with hope and excitement. If I could have my way without repercussions, I would have sent Abbey Leigh on her way immediately.

From that point forward we started relating to each other in a kind of relationship haiku. No wasted words. But there were to be no more sexual high jinks. Abbey Leigh came down with a urinary tract infection that invaded her kidneys and that nearly required hospitalization. She was bedridden with a fever and chills for the better part of three weeks, effectively ending her pursuit of acting work for the remainder of her stay. I helped nurse her back to health between my appointments, unsure as to whether the infection was the result of the amount of sex we'd had, her shower floor sitting, or merely a fluke. She became gentle as a kitten, either from the illness or her own sense of sadness, and we lived out our remaining days in a kind of death row calendar countdown. Only, instead of suffering execution, on the final day I was to be set free.

Abbey Leigh's departure day arrived and I took her to the airport, eager to be on my own. I had it in my mind that, once she was gone, I'd feel released and unburdened. But I'd deceived myself. The moment she waved apologetically and vanished into the crowd I felt abject loneliness. And failure. Abbey Leigh had tried to have a relationship in Los Angeles, while I'd continued to see it as an "experiment." No matter how limited her abilities were, hers was the more sensible attempt. A relationship is a concrete goal. I don't know how you have an "experiment" with someone. I'd failed, once again, to accept and love another human being as she was, for both her strengths and her vulnerabilities. I'd failed to grow into the man I'd expected to become. I'd failed to live up to any of the promises I'd made to myself years before. The only thing I hadn't failed at, it seemed, was simply managing to stay alive.

I hadn't realized how much my connection to Abbey Leigh had sustained me, just as I hadn't realized the same thing about every one of the significant relationships I'd had my whole life. As long as I was engaged in battles with Abbey Leigh, I was engaged with someone who, however awkwardly she might have shown it, cared for me. That's what I'd been aching for: someone to care for, and someone who cared for me. Instead I'd hit a brick wall. This time I'd hit it far from home, with someone who was even farther from hers.

I closed up the rented L.A. apartment and flew back to New York to begin living again in my own place. I was forty years old, the age I thought I'd never reach. I was unmarried, I was on my own, and I was alone.

Medicine Man

FOR A PERIOD of six years I was treated by a psychiatrist who goes by the name of Dr. Loopy. That's not how it's spelled, but it is how it's pronounced. I'm aware of the fact that a certain segment of the population might refuse to see this doctor based on that information alone. Were I asked to predict my own behavior I would almost certainly place myself into that group. The happy fact is that Dr. Loopy is a master of his craft. This happy fact was tempered, somewhat, by a less happy fact: Dr. Loopy charged me $200 per session. Which meant that, throughout my therapy, I got to spend a certain number of hours (and dollars) discussing with Dr. Loopy how trapped and angry I felt about spending so many hours (and dollars) telling him how trapped and angry I felt. Seeing Dr. Loopy was the therapeutic equivalent of living inside an Escher drawing.

Dr. Loopy is the best psychotherapist I've worked with, and I've worked with a few. His insights were well considered, his patience admirable. Still, I doubt our work together has been of tremendous help to me. When it comes to psychotherapy, I'm not sure I'm very good at it. I'm not even convinced I still believe in psychotherapy as the transformational tool I once imagined it to be.

I first came to Dr. Loopy years before meeting Patricia, while in the midst of a burgeoning sexual compulsion. The compulsion I'm referring to had nothing to do with direct contact with another human being. It started around the time I purchased my first laptop computer and logged onto America Online, that family-friendly Internet access system with the cartoon-logo interface. I immediately started spending hour after hour, for months and months, in various chat rooms typing messages back and forth with an assortment of chat "buddies." Rooms with titles ranging from "self pleasure" to "submissive f 4m"; from "I'm pulling it now" to "I Want Daddy for Pleasure." To me, the most pleasing—and puzzling—was "Millionaire for Female."

These chat rooms were stocked with lying men and gullible women, and probably a good number of the reverse. They were but a few of the hundreds of choices awaiting the inquisitive. Or the perverted, depending on your point of view. I struck up private, instant message conversations with hundreds of supposedly female chat room inhabitants. I was regaled with tales of bisexual experimentation; of partner swapping with strangers; of meeting and coupling in bus stations, airports, parks, and alleyways; of fantasies of being impaled on sharp spears; and of elaborate efforts made to enable taking their friends' dogs deep into the woods for an unhurried fuck. As far as entertainment value went, it sure beat the hell out of the six o'clock news. Over the course of a couple of years I wound up having heard it all. More than my share; more than I was comfortable with; more, in the heat of my own morbid passions, than I wish I had ever known existed. Still, I found myself compelled to go back.

I was once told, less than twenty minutes after typing to someone, what a good friend I was. That I was someone's *best* friend, someone who could really be trusted. At times I was told that *while pretending to be someone I wasn't.* I was fascinated by the craving for acceptance expressed by the people I encountered. I was stunned by the depth of their need, and the recklessness it led to. I was baffled, and appalled, at how they could experience the world as the benevolent place they apparently did, after already being driven to such an impersonal arena in their quest for understanding. How did they convince them-selves of my sincerity after five minutes when they'd spent eighteen, twenty-three, forty-five years failing to locate it until then in their own lives? What were they hoping for when they logged on in the morning for their marathon sessions? When they'd send me their phone numbers and invite me to call? When they asked if I'd like to meet? When they offered to fly themselves to wherever I was and wait naked in an unlocked hotel room wearing only a blindfold so I could do whatever I wanted to them? Who were these women who were either unable to acknowledge the dangers of the world they lived in, or willing to risk their lives in pursuit of pleasure, of relief, of debase-ment, of humiliation, of whatever apparently feels like love and closeness to them? Then there was the most frightening question of all. The question that drove me to see Dr. Loopy in the first place. What, sweet Jesus, was I doing in there with them?

DR. LOOPY WAS helpful in gaining some insight. He was helpful when he refused to accept my explanation that I was simply investigating an interesting avenue for material to write about—though I still think of that as a damn good excuse (not to mention good subject matter). But my work with Dr. Loopy was thrown into crisis when, in the midst of our discussions of my Internet adventures, I started running into him every day at the gym. Not for our scheduled sessions, mind you. We just both happened to exercise—and undress, and shower—there.

The first time I saw Dr. Loopy at the gym I was just entering the locker room as he was walking out. I stopped dead in my tracks, did a double take, and sputtered out, "Hey . . ." I'm not sure whether that syllable was intended as a substitute for the word "hello," or whether it was the beginning of a sentence that would have ended with ". . . what the fuck???" I got into my shorts and T-shirt, walked up a couple of flights of stairs, and found myself faced with the choice of hopping on the treadmill next to my psychiatrist, or altering my workout routine by switching to the StairMaster.

Ultimately I sneaked away to exercise on another floor. Though "ultimately" is the wrong word. Because "ultimately" what I did was learn my psychiatrist's workout routine and avoid being at the gym during those hours. When it became clear that the hours he used the gym were the most convenient for me, I took up jogging around the reservoir in Central Park. My discomfort after our first encounter was extreme. But as Dr. Loopy began to ask about my thoughts surrounding our meeting, my discomfort only grew. And grew. And grew.

I first talked about self-consciousness and competition. I described my feelings of inadequacy in terms of my physical condition. Those topics were all vivid enough. But Dr. Loopy, being the skilled fellow he is, continued to probe for the deeper fears that fueled those concerns. It wasn't long before Dr. Loopy and I were back where we'd run into each other in the first place: the locker room.

We talked about nudity, about what made me uneasy about it, and what made me uneasy about it in terms of my psychiatrist.

"Have you had any fantasies about it?" Dr. Loopy asked.

We'd used the term "fantasy," to this point, in contexts that were primarily nonsexual. The term was used simply to explore what kinds of things I imagined might occur in any given situation. But my thought process at that moment went like this: "Oh, I wonder if he's asking me whether I've ever had sexual fantasies about him"; then, "I wonder if it's appropriate for a psychiatrist to ask whether I've had sexual fantasies about him"; "I wonder, if I'd had them, whether I'd tell him that I had"; and, "If I had, and I wouldn't tell him, then what the hell am I here paying two hundred dollars a session for in the first place?" In the midst of those questions running through my mind, which were running through my mind only as a result of the question Dr. Loopy had posed, I had my very first, momentary flash of a sexual image involving Dr. Loopy and myself. Then I wondered, since it had only occurred after Dr. Loopy's prompting, whether or not it counted.

I figured if it was a thought I'd conjured it had its place. I told Dr. Loopy about it, and that's when things really went haywire. Once I'd shared with Dr. Loopy the image that had flashed through my mind, our brief glimpses of each other at the gym only felt like greater humiliations. Now it wasn't just a case of what I might have been thinking. Now I knew that Dr. Loopy *knew* what I was thinking. That only made me start thinking it more. Like the feeling you get when you walk out of a store without buying anything, worrying whether the owners will think you've been stealing; like the way I'll worry, when surrounded by people of another race, whether they think I'm a bigot. I started conjuring sexual images of Dr. Loopy whenever I was in his presence. And I became angry, because I felt the origin of the thoughts didn't lie with me, but that they grew out of his suggestion.

To recap, I was now having recurring sexual thoughts about Dr. Loopy whenever I was in his presence, accompanied by the fear that he knew what I was thinking as I was thinking it. I thought he knew what I was thinking because I thought he's the one who planted the thoughts in my brain to begin with. Not only did I think he knew what I was thinking, but I felt guilty about keeping the thoughts he had planted, and that he knew were in my brain, to myself. Was this progress? I wondered.

OCCASIONALLY, before ushering me into his office, Dr. Loopy would excuse himself and disappear through a doorway into a section of the converted apartment I was unfamiliar with. I'd never contemplated what these delays had meant before. I now started imagining he was using the bathroom, and extrapolating on how that would require his touching his penis during his absence. I'd find myself trying to imagine Dr. Loopy's penis even as I tried to stop myself from imaging his penis, all the while convinced that the only reason I was thinking about Dr. Loopy's penis was because of Dr. Loopy's suggestion that I might have already been thinking about his penis. Then I'd skulk into his office and spend the next hour talking about my mother.

When it comes to psychotherapy, I'm not sure I'm very good at it.

I WENT TO Dr. Loopy to confront my obsessive online behavior, but the issues we wrestled with quickly broadened. I was among a tiny number who had ever survived what I'd been through years before. I was still having trouble adjusting to my status as a living human being. I knew I was a lucky man. But the trial had been costly, and losing the years from ages twenty-four to twenty-nine had set me back in comparison to those I'd started out with. I felt bitter about what I'd been forced to endure, and about what had been lost. I was a man whose life was filled with gifts and riches, but I still felt like I'd been robbed.

"You expect too much," Dr. Loopy said. This was also Dr. Loopy's response in regard to my complaints about Patricia.

"She won't communicate with me," I'd say. Though the more correct representation would have been that she wasn't able to.

Patricia is a person who considers the personal to be private. She'll be horrified by my exposure of any details of our time together. I know this because she did become furious at me for talking about details of our life in private sessions with my psychiatrist, *who's bound by law to keep it all to himself.*

"In my family," Patricia once told me, "when there's a problem, we lift up the corner of a rug, open the cover of a can sunk into the floor, sweep everything into the can, put back the lid, and seal it up tight. We put the rug back in place, and make believe the problem was never there in the first place."

It was all I could do to stop myself from gasping. Patricia had said it with a half chuckle, as if she knew it was kind of crazy. But the half that wasn't chuckling still seemed to think it was a pretty good strategy. The only way I know how to relate to people is through direct communication. Patricia and I were headed for a collision somewhere down the line.

In spite of these warnings I'd already been considering asking Patricia to marry me. I was proud of myself for having stuck with the relationship with the level of commitment I'd brought to it so far. I was determined to work my way past what I'd come to see (with what I took as Dr. Loopy's approval) as my own inability to accept the limitations of others. But there were some crevasses on the landscape I couldn't leave unexplored.

Patricia had given me hazy indications that there were events in her past that she seemed to find troubling, but she wasn't willing to recount them. She told me she was bothered by thoughts and memories that felt too large and frightening for her to confront, but she would not consider talking about them with me or with a professional. She wouldn't even tell me what they were. Whenever I broached any of the topics I thought couples considering the considerable step of marriage ought to discuss, like finances, child rearing, religion, or aging parents, Patricia met my inquiries with ferocious resistance.

"I feel like you're testing me," she complained.

"No. I'm trying to get to *know* you," I responded. "I'm trying to get to know how you feel about things, how you handle things, how you think people should interact and share information and responsibilities. That's how people can tell if they're compatible."

"You see," she said. "You *are* testing me. What if I don't give the right answers? You might decide you don't want to be with me."

I never knew how to answer this. It always seemed to be the ultimate trapdoor question. I tried to answer honestly, but also lovingly and reassuringly.

"But that's what people *do*. They investigate. They *talk*. And then, yes, they decide. But what I can say is that I hope—whatever gets said, and whatever gets revealed—that we continue to decide we want to be together. Maybe even want to be together all the more."

"I just think it's a leap of faith," Patricia insisted. "If you love someone, you trust that you'll find a way to solve whatever problems come up. You can't think up every problem in advance. You cross those bridges when you come to them."

Upon hearing this exchange, Dr. Loopy gave me one of my favorite tidbits of his insight.

"What I'm getting," he told me, "is that you see a bridge in front of you."

And I did. But it was the rickety, handmade-footbridge variety, like in a jungle adventure movie, with lots of slats missing.

These were the early days of my psychotherapy with Dr. Loopy, long before I'd first traveled to Australia and met Abbey Leigh. I was dutifully trekking to his office once or twice a week, giving it the yeoman's try to stop feeling cheated, and to learn to appreciate the abundance of goodness life had already offered me.

"You expect too much," he continued to say.

Patricia is a good, loving woman, I told myself in response. I'd underappreciated some very good women already. When Patricia became rigid in the face of my attempts to break through her barriers, I backed off.

If she feels too nervous under pressure, I thought, then maybe taking the pressure off might work. Maybe if I gave her a stronger sense of commitment, she might feel secure enough to open up. I asked Patricia to marry me, and she said yes.

I HAVE NO illusions now that those were the best motives for proposing marriage. I'm pretty sure they're not the worst ones, either. But the idea didn't prove to be good, or effective. Our fights escalated, and our household became increasingly tense.

"I feel like you're asking me to buy a house," I finally said, in a moment of frustration sometime after our engagement. "I'll put my entire life savings into it, and I'll promise to live in the house for the rest of my life. But the agreement you're insisting on is that I can only see the rooms on the ground floor, even though there are two more floors upstairs. Whatever's inside those rooms is off-limits until after I move in, and no matter what I might find up there, I've already agreed I'll never move out."

In case it's not clear, if you ever find yourself saying anything like that to anyone, especially a fiancée, it's time to pack up the tent and leave town. The show is over, and there won't be any encores. But that doesn't mean the third act won't stretch on for another year or two.

The relationship was then extended, and eventually doomed, by my absence. I spent seven months making a television show in Los Angeles, two months at home, and then two months shooting the movie in Australia, where I met Abbey Leigh. That's a spell of nine out of eleven months apart. While I was in Los Angeles, Patricia visited once. While I was in Australia, as every other actor's spouse came and went, Patricia opted to stay home because of her terror of flying even the shortest distances.

I was going out of my mind. I was frustrated by my relationship at home, but forbidden to pursue anything else while away. I ached for some form of erotic attachment to see me through our extensive separations. After building up my courage to ask directly for what I wanted—and, though it might sound silly, what I felt I *needed* to stay connected—Patricia decided that she didn't enjoy phone sex, or even talking about sex over the telephone. That's when I met the twenty-five-year-old Australian. She was a young woman who possessed not only beauty but an uncanny honesty, forthrightness, and interest in exploring her own emotional life and the motivations of those around her. I spent a tender and torturous two months falling in love behind my fiancée's back, doing my best to keep my hands off the woman I felt compelled to spend all my time with.

"I don't want to have anything to confess when I get home," I told everyone around, who could easily see what was happening. "I want to be able to say, 'Don't worry, honey. It was only emotional.'"

I had myself locked down in a prison of my own making. I was getting none of what I wanted, and doing no one else any good. The conflicts were my own. But a good deal of my paralysis stemmed from trying to live up to the lessons I thought I'd learned in psychotherapy about my overdeveloped sense of entitlement.

"You expect too much," Dr. Loopy had said.

Which might have been true. But I sure needed more than what I was getting.

BACK HOME IN New York after meeting Abbey Leigh, I resumed my psychotherapy sessions. For fifty minutes two or three times a week, I obsessed. Through agonized hour-long phone calls with friends, over every meal at a restaurant with anyone, and every step of the way around the Central Park reservoir, I bombarded myself, and whoever was with me, with my dilemma. Should I stay or should I go? Was it right to override all my concerns and marry Patricia? Or should I do what I'd already determined was my pattern thus far by (God, forgive me) trading up for a better model?

Those are good questions to ask, if they accurately identify the problem. But what if a person, like me, really did suffer from an inability to appreciate the privileges and people in his life, like Dr. Loopy suggested—but *really was with the wrong person*? At the least, one might become confused. If you were me, you'd become profoundly depressed.

. . .

THE TOPIC OF antidepressant medication had been brought up by every one of the therapists I'd seen over the years. But the conversations had always seemed rote, as if it were an option that had to be discussed and dispensed with, so the real "treatment" could begin. I'd quickly expressed my reluctance to taking any unnecessary medication, my concerns about antidepressant medication and their side effects in particular, as well as my belief that I wasn't depressed enough to need it. (This has since made me question—in direct contradiction to my general views on medical self-determination— whether a depressed person would be the best judge of whether or not he's depressed enough to need chemical interventions.)

My psychiatrists all concurred with my assessment. We then launched into the laborious and surreal process of my telling my life story to a string of medically certified strangers. Due to the particulars of my story, this recounting would be like a horror movie highlight reel. The experience would be just depressing enough to make me leave the psychiatrist's office aching for another appointment.

I'd sailed through my years of treatments, recurrences, and recoveries from acute leukemia without any psychotropic medication. I'd survived the breakup with Jackie, the girlfriend of five years who'd nursed me through the illness, without it. I'd stumbled through my post-leukemia life and relationships with my dopamine and serotonin levels unaltered from their default concentrations. I'd continued to hold off throughout the year of tormenting myself and two different women on two separate continents. I'd remained unmedicated while I lived in Los Angeles with Abbey Leigh, relishing our sexual exploits but simply reversing the roles I'd assigned the two women by missing the familiarity of Patricia while alternately fucking or having screaming fights with her Australian counterpart. I bounced like a pinball with limited human awareness from one entanglement to another, either with women I'd already been involved with, or ones I hadn't yet pushed completely away, without ingesting any prescription medication. Only after the terrorist attack on New York in September 2001, after Patricia and I had taken yet another failed shot at reconciliation; only after I'd visited Sotheby's and sold off the engagement ring, and after Abbey Leigh chose to decline yet another of my back-and-forth approaches in which I asked if I could come see her again in Australia; only after I'd been left completely alone in what, at the time, felt like the loneliest city in the United States did I find myself starting off my psychotherapy session unable to speak, and able only to cry. I told Dr. Loopy I felt that I couldn't function, and that I needed some help that involved more than just talk. We discussed the pharmaceutical options, a drug was decided upon, and I started taking the pills.

SOMETIME BEFORE MY surrender to the medication Patricia and I attended some agonizing "couples therapy" sessions together. Part of the reason they were agonizing (and doomed to fail) was my inability to confess my ongoing infatuation with another woman, in another hemisphere. During our last session Patricia said something terrifically astute.

"I don't think Evan really loves me," she said. "I think he *values* me. I think he respects me, and values my devotion. Evan loves *qualities* about me. But I don't think he really loves me, for just *being* me."

Patricia was equating "love" with "enjoyment," as opposed to what I'd usually thought of as the more substantial aspects she'd dismissed: respect, value, loyalty, devotion. As if being "enjoyed" was even more important.

And she was right. I loved Patricia emotionally, but for intellectualized reasons. And that wasn't enough for her, as it shouldn't have been for either of us. As true as it can be that good sex, or fun and excitement, might not be enough to keep people together without shared core values, the cruel hoax with Patricia and me turned out to be that the opposite was just as true. Shared values and moral convictions aren't enough if you don't enjoy the same things, or don't have fun in the same ways. Patricia was the one who finally decided we shouldn't be living together, or even seeing each other. She could no longer imagine us having a life together.

"I can't see it, and I don't want it," she said.

She might not have been able to discuss the issues very well, but when it came time to say what should have been said long before, she was more capable than I. This led to my becoming sure that I'd made a terrible mistake and absolutely had to have her back.

"I can't see it, and I don't want it," Patricia said. But she had ended the conversation with words I'd often used in such situations, either to soften a blow or to protect my own possible future interests: "At least not right now."

To a man as confused as I was, that could easily be taken as meaning, "You know, unless I change my mind—like you keep doing—sometime soon."

BEFORE STARTING THE antidepressant medication I spent weeks crying. I fell into a state of entrenched sadness that I'd never encountered before. I've come across the clichéd phrase describing depression as "falling into a pit." Like a lot of clichés, I've found it to be based on truth. I felt submerged, that I could hear life going on somewhere above me, and see light from somewhere beyond my reach. Even in the depths of illness I'd never felt so without ability to plot a course back to the land of the living.

Over these days I wasn't able to erase Patricia's parting words from my mind: "At least not right now." I'd been spending sleepless nights in imaginary discussions with her for weeks since our last conversation. Against my psychiatrist's advice I dialed her up. I asked whether she might have any inklings of desire to ever try again. She was surprised to hear my voice, and seemed even more surprised by my question.

"No, Evan," she said. "I thought I was really clear. I'm sorry. I didn't mean to leave open the possibility of trying again. It's not something I've been thinking about, and it's not something I want to do."

This time she didn't end with "At least not right now." This time, that was it.

I hung up the phone, and I fell apart. I sobbed and sobbed, sitting on the edge of the bed we'd shared. I cursed myself for setting myself back again. I wondered how long it would take, this time, to pull myself up, and out. The answer arrived exactly ten minutes later when I stopped crying and never felt so sad again.

I immediately thought about the medication. It had to have been the medication. Something had happened to me that—rightfully or wrongfully—felt crushing, and I'd simply felt sad for a period of minutes. That kind of transition had never happened for me before. In fact, the crying switched off so suddenly I was concerned. I felt so well and pain-free I thought there must be something wrong. I decided to perform my own psychological test.

I'd been a basket case for weeks, unable to think about Patricia without experiencing agonizing pain. I'd had to wrestle my thoughts to keep them from wandering toward her in order to keep myself from tearing over. I decided to purposely push my thoughts toward her. Not only that, but to push them toward the most painful, regret-filled memories I could conjure. As hard as I tried that day, and over the days and weeks to come, *I could not make myself feel sad.*

This is precisely what I'd been assured the medication was not capable of accomplishing. It's what I'd always heard was beyond its potential. But I can tell you, whatever it might have ever done for anyone else, it did it for me. It did it completely. It did it absolutely. It freaked me out. But after feeling as sad as I had for as long as I had, I didn't mind one bit.

Besides setting a hard floor beyond which my emotions were not capable of falling, the drug's sudden onset also lifted my baseline mood tremendously. I found myself walking the streets of New York with an inexplicable smile on my face just minutes after feeling awful and blue as a result of Patricia's finally breaking things off with me. I felt contented, enthusiastic, and in possession of an energetic curiosity about everything around me. I'd never had a feeling like it before. I'd known happiness and I'd known euphoria, but only the kind that resulted from something specific and pleasant occurring. I had never known just feeling good for no apparent reason.

I found this fascinating. I had spent nearly every moment of my life wondering why almost everyone around me seemed so much more optimistic than I was about everything. I'd mocked—both privately and publicly—what I'd experienced as the naïve cheerleading I'd encountered in all my collaborative endeavors, finding others foolish for their enthusiasm. In one crashing moment of realization, I learned that most of the people I'd come across lived their lives in a profoundly different emotional state than I had walked around with for as long as I could remember. So this is how all those silly people I've made fun of must feel all the time, I thought. But if they're happy and having a good time, while I'm feeling miserable and superior, who's the silly one?

I TOOK ANTIDEPRESSANT medication for only seven months. The experience so profoundly altered my perceptions that I credit the medication for much of my recovery, and much of the contentment that followed. I've heard depression described as "anger turned inward." I didn't find this to be the case. My anger (in case you haven't noticed) points straight out. I've also heard it described as "grief out of proportion to circumstance." I prefer this assessment, because "proportion" has to do with "perspective," and the medication permanently altered mine.

I got to feel, for the first time, what it's like to walk through a day with a different chemical cocktail bathing my brain. I was transformed into an innately happier creature as a result of it. The knowledge of that less burdened state has lived on in my memory long after I chose to discontinue the medication. A person doesn't need to hold a newborn baby to know how wonderful holding a baby feels. The memory endures, and the ability to conjure the sensation from that memory exists. Simply releasing my mind from its constraints for a few months gave me an awareness of an emotional state I hadn't known was possible. Once I'd tasted that sweeter existence, even one that was a result of pharmaceutical manipulation, I found my mind was able to aim toward, and reach, that brighter light on its own.

"You expect too much," Dr. Loopy had said. Maybe he was right. Still, I discovered more than I knew was possible.

The suddenness of the shift made me question my belief in psychotherapy as a curative tool. I still recommend it wholeheartedly as a way to understand oneself better, and as an aid in relating to and getting along with others. But I'll never depend on it to address another depression. For that I'll take a pill. Pills gave me my first glimpse out of the hole I was stuck in, and my first glimpse back into the hole from a different place than the bottom of it. I can only wonder how different things might have been had I taken them a lot sooner than I did.

Thanksgiving Days

THANKSGIVING IS MY favorite holiday. It always has been. That might seem strange to hear from a man like me. But throughout my entire life—since long before leukemia impinged upon it—it's been the holiday that's made the most sense.

It's a less overtly "religious" holiday than most others celebrated in the United States, but it still possesses significant spiritual heft. That's kept it the one holiday my family feels most safely secular in celebrating. But my attachment goes beyond that. It's the one day I've felt free to shed whatever inhibitions I've had in regard to indulging in and displaying gratitude.

Why the inhibition? Has it been a defense against getting my hopes up? If so, the tactic merely ensures that instead of suffering disappointment as a *result* of anything, disappointment will be the precursor *to* everything. The only guarantee there is that I'll cause myself the pain I'm afraid others might inflict.

Gratitude is the mind-set that allowed me to save my life years ago.

When I was newly diagnosed with leukemia, I had to consciously construct a fortress of gratitude from which to battle the overwhelming urge to squander my energies on an unending series of temper tantrums. I threw my share of tantrums all the same. I was an angrier young man than most of my friends and family knew how to deal with. But I managed to convince myself, from my muscles to my soul (and against much evidence), that I was a blessed man, and that each day of life was a gift to be cherished. How far I've drifted since then.

November '02

Elisa Atti, an Italian-born scientist who's been in the United States barely two years, and who studies bone biology at Hospital for Special Surgery in New York, has joined the Handler family for her first (and my forty-first) Thanksgiving celebration. Elisa and I had our first official "date" only six weeks before her first Thanksgiving expedition. We've been living on opposite coasts since we met, she in New York, and I in California, where I moved not long ago. She's come to North Carolina—where I've just had knee surgery to repair a torn meniscus—to nurse me, to care for me, and to join close to fifty Jews in overeating what will seem to her some of the most puzzling food combinations she's ever encountered.

I don't know how other families handle their annual rituals (and I've never much enjoyed trying to fit into the well-cemented traditions of families other than my own). But in my family the dinner varies as its venue switches from year to year. There have been gourmet feasts carefully handcrafted by one family member acting as the lone chef. There have been rockier potluck dinners. In more recent years there have been dinners trucked in by extrafamilial vendors. Elisa's first American Thanksgiving dinner is the largest and loudest we've ever put together, as it's being held over the same weekend we're celebrating my parents' fiftieth wedding anniversary. If my crutches, electronic ice packs, and medical nightmare flashbacks aren't enough to frighten away my new Bolognese girlfriend, if she's not put off by the propensity toward obesity she'll witness within my genetic pool (or the inability nearly every one of us has to resist interrupting everyone else mid-sentence), this dinner will introduce her to canned cranberry sauce—still bearing the shape and imprints of the interior of the can—rather than fresh homemade. There will be melted marshmallows—a food substance I can't figure out how to explain to her, and which still makes no sense to her (or me) once I've succeeded—mixed in with the sweet potatoes. There will be a fully grown man who was born out of wedlock to his abundantly tattooed mother, who has herself become a grandmother at the age of thirty-nine. We're Jews from the Northeast, but that doesn't make us much different from southern white trash (no offense to the South, the Northeast, the white race, Jews, any of my immediate or extended family, or trash of any kind intended).

ELISA HAD ALREADY been making me laugh constantly—sometimes purposefully, sometimes not. Over the first few days we spent together she offhandedly dismissed the mime master Marcel Marceau, whom she'd seen perform once in Bologna, and who had, apparently, bored her to tears.

"Okay, he's a legend. I know," Elisa said. "But come on. Ten minutes, maybe."

I adored her enthusiasm over a compliment tossed her way at an entertainment industry event by the completely Caucasian fashion designer Isaac Mizrahi. He told her she has beautiful eyebrows and hair. As he walked away she whispered to me, "What kind of name is that? Mizrahi?"

"I don't know," I said. "Israeli, I guess."

"Oh," Elisa replied, all seriousness. "I thought it was Japanese."

Elisa can sometimes fail to comprehend anything but the most straightforward English language communication, yet perceive everything within the most imagistic transmission. It can take six tries to get through a simple "What would you like to have for dinner?" conversation. Then she'll glance at the lyrics to a Randy Newman song and say, as if she's the first to make the discovery, "This man is a genius."

Within ten glorious days—all spent having a whirlwind adventure in a luxurious Manhattan hotel—we made plans to travel together to visit my parents in North Carolina for Thanksgiving and to stay with her parents over Christmas in Bologna, Italy. I think I was getting the better end of that deal.

It was barely October and we'd already made plans that took us through the beginning of January. I jokingly suggested we make a commitment to stay together at least three months, so as not to lose any money on nonrefundable airfares. Over the next few days we playfully refined our agreement. If, after three months together, we still wanted to stay a couple, we'd sign on for a second three-month term. If, at the end of the second three months, we again wanted to re-up, we'd promise to double the time frame and stick it out for a six-month segment. If, at the end of that—which by then would have kept us together for a year—we were still happy with each other, then we'd promise to stay together for the rest of our lives. A perfect progression: ten days of bliss; three-month commitment; three-month commitment; six-month commitment; eternity. Here's to the next six months, and wherever we might end up after that.

January '03

Some weeks after we visited our families, Elisa and I met in a neutral corner to grab a few more days together. This time, being the orthopedic researcher she is, she was attending a "Bone Meeting" in Montreal. Since I had a couple of days free, I flew from Los Angeles to eastern Canada to be with her.

Our second night in Montreal we attended one of the conference meetings with Elisa's colleagues. We were fed from utilitarian warming trays in a standard hotel meeting room. After the meal we were entertained by a circus act in which a woman who'd had three of her vertebrae replaced with metal substitutes performed acrobatics between the dinner tables. As she tumbled and flipped, X-rays of her spine were projected onto a screen at the front of the room below the name of the implant's manufacturer. The spectacles occurring at professional conferences around the world surpass the offspring of the most fecund imaginations.

In Elisa's hotel room later that night I leafed through a magazine. Offhandedly I tossed an insult toward an actress whose photo was featured.

"Look at that," I said. "She's getting another movie produced based on her magnificent breasts."

"Do you think she has magnificent breasts?" Elisa asked.

I was startled not so much by the question as the tone of her voice. I looked up to see an expression on Elisa's face I'd never seen before.

"Why don't you go out with her, then, if you think her breasts are so magnificent?"

I thought she must have been kidding, so I laughed.

"Oh, you think it's funny?" Elisa went on. "Why don't you go laugh with your actress and her magnificent breasts? I'm sure she'll think you're very funny."

"Elisa, I don't even know this woman," I said. Then I realized that was beside the point. "What's going on here? I've come to see you. I've traveled three thousand miles to Montreal in the middle of the winter to see you. Why are you upset about something I said about a photo in a magazine?"

"Oh, I didn't realize it was such a hardship for you to come and see me. Next time don't bother. You can go see your movie star girlfriend with her magnificent brea—"

"Stop with the magnificent breasts. I'm sorry I said it. But what's going on? Why are you so upset?"

This was my first experience with a side of Elisa I hadn't encountered before. I hate to admit to the stereotyping I'm guilty of by saying so, but I've come to refer to it as her "going Italian" on me. Out of nowhere, for reasons either justified or absurd, Elisa's jealousy will rear up and render her unrecognizable—unless, that is, you're looking for Mariangela Melato in the Lina Wertmüller film *Swept Away*. In that case, you'd recognize her right away.

I'd thought, until that moment, that I'd discovered the perfect partner. We'd only been seeing each other sporadically over the course of a couple of months. We still lived on opposite coasts. But I'd allowed myself to imagine a conflict-free progression toward a blissful future. I tried to joke with her, I tried to explain the logic of my attempt to impugn the talent of the actress in the photograph, and I apologized for my insensitivity. Nothing I said could loosen the grip of Elisa's jealousy.

"If you want to insult someone, you don't talk about her magnificent breasts," she said. "I don't think you wanted to insult her. I think you must want to be with her. Go, if that's what you want. You don't have to stay here with me. Go be with the movie star with the magnificent breasts."

The next day I flew back to Los Angeles wondering if the whole thing had been a dream. Or two dreams. The delightful dream of Elisa and me falling in love, and the nightmare of the Montreal meltdown. I didn't know which one was the reality and which the aberration.

November '03
The problem with predictions, or blueprints, is that they don't allow for improvisation. Anyone who's ever tried to meld two lives into a single unit knows the infinite opportunities for complications. Coupling up is far more complicated than adding one and one.

Which is one of the many reasons I'm still so glad I found Elisa. Did we fail to stick with our planned progression of commitment? We did. But we failed by moving faster than planned, faster than I would have predicted, faster than I'd ever thought I would, and faster than I'd recommend anyone else try.

Elisa will now join me again for her sophomore (and my forty-second) Thanksgiving celebration. This time we'll be at my sister's home, in another state than the year before, with only twelve in attendance. Instead of traveling six weeks after meeting each other, we'll now be traveling six weeks after our wedding at our favorite restaurant in New York. Our legal legitimization of our commitment came right on schedule. Our wedding day fell just four days short of our one-year-and-ten-day target. But we committed ourselves to its implementation months before we'd originally, and jokingly, intended.

As our clash in Montreal showed, our march toward the aisle wasn't completely free of conflict. In years past my instinct would have been to head for the hills after such an episode. But I'd already sensed enough about Elisa, and been able to accurately measure the depth of her value to me, to stay in the ring another few rounds. I was shaken by the revelation of her insecurity. I was equally shaken to recognize the aspects of my personality that tend to provoke it. But the happiest discovery was that, for all the potential explosiveness of the combination, Elisa and I knew how to defuse the flare-ups before they became unmanageable. Once upon a time I would have taken the stand that I shouldn't have to work so hard to convince my lover of my devotion. With Elisa, I made it my mission simply to help her feel as secure and well loved as I could. Sometimes the way to accomplish that was to keep my mouth shut.

No ONE WHO celebrates his first wedding at the age of forty-two completely escapes the embarrassments of late bachelorhood. For me the lowlight was my fortieth birthday party. It was a sparsely populated event. This was in spite of the fact that I stretched my address book to its limit by inviting a score of people I was no longer even close to. Several of the guests were women I'd had failed relationships with. And, of course, I came to the party—and left—alone. Still, waiting so long to pledge myself to someone has had tremendous benefits.

I can't speak with authority on the emotional maturity of anyone other than myself, but I know one thing for certain: I got married as an adult. That wouldn't have been the case had I gotten married at twenty-five, and it wouldn't have been the case had I gotten married at thirty. I don't think I qualified as a child at thirty-five, but that doesn't mean I was all grown up, either. I might have been mature at thirty-nine, but the woman I almost married at that age wasn't—which calls into question the very maturity I just bestowed upon myself. The point is, I got married exactly when I was meant to, and not a second later than when I was prepared to handle it.

Elisa and I wanted confirmation of our compatibility to come quickly. There were some odd sensations that resulted from rushing headlong into a love we both felt relieved to have found. If we barely knew each other at all in Montreal, we'd only had ten months' more experience with each other the day we got married.

"Almost everyone I know, I know better than you," my wife quipped on our wedding night. Still, I had not a molecule of doubt that we'd done the right thing.

Whenever the topic of my parents' wedding comes up, my father is quick to state he had no idea what was going on. He was twenty-four years old and his bride was all of twenty. As he tells it, he was more bystander than planner or participant—unless you count choosing your bride as part of the wedding plans. Since they've now passed their fifty-fifth anniversary and are still happy to have each other, it could be argued that was the most crucial aspect of the event.

Elisa and I were more fortunate than that. Being adults with adequate incomes, and being adults who enjoy independence from our families, we crafted the wedding of our choice. We wrote our own vows, interviewed and chose our own official, made up our own guest list, chose the venue and the menu, and succeeded in creating the event that most perfectly pleased us.

I approached Tom Valenti, a top New York chef and restaurateur, even though I thought it would be impossible to have our wedding at his newest restaurant on New York's Upper West Side. Ouest had become my favorite restaurant in the city, and it was the spot where Elisa and I had ended our first date. I was surprised to learn that by holding the wedding on a Sunday morning and early afternoon we'd be able to have Chef Valenti's fabulous food and elegant room for a fraction of the cost of the factory-style banquet halls we'd visited.

Ouest's main room is laid out with deep red circular leather booths and banquettes and giant Art Deco–style chandeliers. Two staircases lead up to railed balconies, each of which gives dramatic views of the main room below. We climbed one of those staircases to stand under a bower of white lilies and recite our vows, every word of which was translated into Italian for Elisa's parents and friends who'd traveled from Italy.

The first sentence of my wedding vows got the biggest laugh I've ever gotten from a crowd in my life.

"Most of those who know me here know me as a man who's been extremely difficult to please," I said.

I went on, speaking to Elisa. "All I ever wanted out of life was to feel like the most privileged man to have ever lived. It didn't seem like so much to ask. Slowly, over time, I learned that it was. Yet, that's exactly how I have felt, every minute of every day, since my first day with you."

We chose our favorite entrees and desserts from the menu and programmed Elisa's iPod with our ideal ideas of background music, which played through the restaurant's sound system. Not a single song played that either one of us didn't want to hear. Not a morsel was served that wasn't to our taste. Not a single person attended as a concession to anyone else. As one of my enjoyably misanthropic friends who flew across the country to be with us said, "It's the perfect wedding. Great food, no dancing."

Dancing or not, it was the best party I've ever been to. It was the most enjoyable five hours of my life.

But having freedom and privilege is meaningless, and provides no joy, if the people getting married don't function as an effective team. Gauging from the subgenre of films and fiction, the number of couples who discover their incompatibility during the planning of their weddings must pass into the tens of millions.

What Elisa and I discovered in the planning, the execution, the enjoyment, and the aftermath of our wedding was that our instincts led us to want to have the same things, and even to do things the same way. In the few instances when our instincts and impulses diverged, we found compromise to be not only easy but joyful. Those might not be completely unique accomplishments, but not everyone is so lucky.

I'd always known Thanksgiving as a day that held its deepest meaning the worse things were in my life. It was a day to remember to be thankful for all the things I was still lucky to have, even after most everything else had been taken away. Now the holiday has been transformed. I get to celebrate, not only the things I feel grateful for, but the fact that I am *already* grateful—and that Gratitude herself exists. I celebrate that I'm lucky enough to have embraced her, and that she has embraced me. She can be a fickle mistress. It's interesting that I've made peace with her as a result of having pledged myself to someone else. Women can be funny that way. Sometimes they're only willing to give themselves to you when you've resigned yourself to their absence. I'm happy to have both of mine, whatever the reasons for their simultaneous appearance. And I'm grateful they're willing to share me the way they do.

Italian Dreaming

WHEN I WAS first shown the collection of buildings my father-in-law owns in Molinella, a small town in northern Italy, I immediately began calculating how much longer he might live. The buildings are not luxurious. Two of the three are what the family call "factories," but they're really just large, rectangular brick and concrete shells on the outskirts of town used by various small manufacturing companies. The interiors resemble nothing so much as enormous garages. One of the factories has a couple of modest apartments attached. Inside one of those apartments is where my wife did most of her growing up.

The third building is in town and has two floors. Downstairs is another garage and a finished rental space that currently houses a local community center. Upstairs is another apartment, and that's where my wife lived—with her parents and her grandmother—until she was nine, when they moved to the factory one-half kilometer away. The apartment in town is also where her father was born.

Shortly after her grandmother's death, twenty-seven years after they'd left, Elisa's parents moved back to the apartment in town. People don't move very much or very far in Italy. In my father-in-law's case they don't move very much or very far, then as soon as possible they move right back where they started.

Since my father-in-law was only sixty-five at the time of my first visit, and since his own mother had lived to ninety-two, things weren't looking immediately promising in terms of my wife's inheritance. Being almost forty-four myself, I realized I might not come into copossession of the estate until I was nearly seventy-five. A depressing thought. But I wasn't sad or frustrated. I simply started to think about leaving my wife for someone else. Which, in case you're even more damaged than I am and need it explained, is much worse.

But that line of thinking is incongruous with my emotional attachment to the people involved. I love my wife madly and deeply, with gusto and delight. Aside from some purely instinctual animalistic urges that arise now and then, I am free from conflict in my devotion to her and my commitment to our union. I've never been able to say anything so decisive about anyone before.

I also love her parents. Ivonne and Umberto are the kindest, most generous, most enjoyable non-English-speaking couple I've ever known. They're among the most enjoyable creatures I've known capable of any kind of speech.

One of the great pleasures of my life with Elisa is getting to know her family, as well as getting to know her home country and culture—though I have found some Italian customs baffling. The cultural habits that foreign travel has made me question the most, though, are those based here in the good old U.S.A.

All through my youth, and even through early adulthood, I lived under the false impression shared by many Americans: that the United States of America is the best at everything, and has the best, most advanced versions of everything. I've got news for you: it's not true.

For instance, if you think the United States leads the world in cleanliness or availability of abundant produce, you haven't visited an Italian grocery store. My wife has said many times upon merely eyeing an American food shop, "An Italian would never buy food from those people. In Italy, those people would be out of business." That was her response to a pretty decent place. I've also seen the look on her parents' faces as they gazed into a New York delicatessen, horrified by the grime on the linoleum floor. The processed, prepackaged food products and the yellowing, crusted "fresh" ones were secondary insults.

But even before I'd had a chance to experience the lifestyles of my wife's Italian compatriots, or to see their reactions to our cities, I learned about their collective fascination with us. The first evening I spent in the presence of Elisa's parents was on a trip we took for Christmas, only two months after we'd begun dating. In spite of her Catholic background and upbringing, in spite of her parents' lifelong indoctrination to ancient small-town customs and habits, and in spite of our unmarried status, there was none of the drama that had accompanied my visits to the ancestral homes of previous girlfriends. Those earlier trips had all been surrounded by seemingly endless negotiations over who'd sleep where. Delicate, roundabout discussions had to be held about how established a relationship needed to be before her parents, or even the girlfriend herself, felt comfortable enough for us to close the door to a room and share a bed.

Neither Elisa nor her parents indulged in such postures. Her parents are working-class Catholics living in a tiny medieval town in northern Italy. But they possess a respect for their only daughter that lifts their sophistication beyond that of many cosmopolitan Americans. When I met Ivonne and Umberto, Elisa's childhood room had been made up for the two of us like a kiddie-porn honeymoon suite. Two single beds had been pushed together and made up as one. The wall above the headboards was covered with framed photos of Elisa at fourteen, fifteen, and sixteen years of age. Across the room were posters of Peter Sellers and Jerry Lewis that had hung there since she'd put them up when she was a teenager. Though many now think I've ended up with a woman as beautiful as my wife because I work in film and television, the truth is that Elisa thinks Jerry Lewis, circa 1965, is the sexiest man she's ever seen.

"He was gorgeous," she says.

In her childhood bedroom I looked at the poster of the Jewish clown grinning like an idiot. It's an odd fetish she's got, I thought. But I'm happy to reap the benefits.

Later, while making love in the room she'd slept in since she was a little girl, I told Elisa how nice it was of her parents to allow me to defile her in her childhood bed.

"What does this word mean?" Elisa asked. "I do not know this word: 'defile.'"

"It means, 'to make dirty,'" I told her.

RELIEVED OF THE need to focus our energies on the avoidance of sex between adult offspring, there was time for talk about other things. This talk consisted mostly of a lengthy list of questions from Elisa's father, mother, and brother, her mother's brother, his wife, and their three adult daughters, her parents' friends and their children, and just about every other Italian I met—all translated by Elisa—about every detail of life in the United States.

Only later would I learn the focus of the greatest amount of Italian inquiry into American life. In spite of differences in diet, health care, and forms of government and jurisprudence, my wife's family and friends' deepest curiosity has to do with how Americans keep their asses clean. In the literal, as opposed to the figurative, sense.

Not that I have tremendous faith in my countrymen's hygienic fastidiousness, but I hadn't realized there was an issue, or how the issue had declared itself internationally. It turns out the intrigue isn't based on actual encounters but on their awareness of the absence of that ubiquitous Italian household appliance: the bidet.

I'd always thought it was the French who most adored bidets. To judge by my wife's family and their friends, the Italians are generally not enamored of their froggy neighbors. But it turns out the bidet is an essential item in every respectable Italian household. The question on a lot of Italians' minds is how Americans can consider themselves respectable—or merely clean—without washing their asses thoroughly after each and every bowel movement.

"How do you do it here?" my wife asked early in our relationship. "Does everyone take a shower every time they go to the bathroom?"

I know they don't, but I didn't see how I could admit it. I felt myself a member of a stinking, feces-ridden people.

I'm not sure I can come up with an explanation. I've tried. I've offered arguments. Firstly, that our toilet paper is better than theirs. It's softer and more absorbent. Or—and this I was reluctant to ask, since it's so graphic and potentially disgusting—it really depends, doesn't it, on the specific nature of each particular bowel movement? But no matter what I say, or no matter what I think but don't say, in the final analysis there's no question at all. No matter what the explanation or rationalization, no matter what my country's reputation for gleaming indoor plumbing and access to hot water and scented soaps, she's right. Washing is cleaner than not washing. You can talk about how Europeans don't shower as often as we do, and they don't. You can talk about their use of deodorant being more parsimonious than ours, and it is. But no matter where the line is drawn, or where your particular sympathies line up, one fact is crystal clear and hard as the hardest stone. Their asses are cleaner than ours. It's as simple as that.

I WAS TALKING this over on the phone recently with my parents (who'd removed a bidet from their new house in order to enlarge the shower) and got some confirmation.

"Washing five times a day *is* cleaner than washing once," my father said. This is the same father who drinks a fiber-fortified cocktail each day to help with the regularity he claims to rarely enjoy. Judging from his "five times a day" comment, perhaps his aspirations for evacuations are unrealistically high.

"But it doesn't matter," he went on. "I don't like the bidet. It tickles."

"No, no, no. You use your *hand,*" instructed my wife, who'd been listening in on an extension. "You don't let the water hit you. You take the water in your hand, and then you wash."

Silence on the line.

I thought, Their asses might be cleaner, but their hands sure can't be. Then I decided to offer a joke.

"The real Italian way to do it is the most effective," I said. "You clean and moisturize together by using a slice of prosciutto."

Everyone laughed. But my wife's eyes grew wide, and she said, "That's not a bad idea!"

Weeks later, Elisa and I were watching an episode of a television show. The scene featured one rendition of a classic American TV joke capitalizing on the sound of a toilet flushing. Immediately after, the husband appears and says good night to his wife.

"You see," Elisa said. "That man is going to bed and he didn't wash his ass."

Shame on him. Shame on us all.

It's not only television characters that have disgusted my wife. Elisa related an instance that had horrified her on a business trip during which she'd been forced to share a queen-size hotel bed with a colleague.

"She used the bathroom before coming to bed," Elisa told me. "You could tell. I don't want to be disgusting, but you know . . . with sounds and the smell. And she didn't take a shower. She just came out, and got into bed next to me."

Elisa shuddered at the memory.

"I don't understand how you can do that. Maybe if you're in the woods. If we were in a tent, okay. But . . ."

When forced to, my industrious wife has even learned to take matters into her own hands. Prior to her confrontation with American realities, Elisa studied for a year in London. There she'd been forced to improvise in another supposedly advanced but unwashed country.

"We didn't have any bidets in the dormitories there, either," Elisa said. "So I would wash my ass in the sink."

Those nasty English get what they deserve.

CULTURAL DIVERGENCES ABOUND. Elisa, and every Italian I've ever spoken with, is horrified by the way American politicians speak about God, and plead with him to bless our nation.

"God bless the United States of America" comes out of our television set whenever a president speaks, and Elisa's head snaps back as if she's been struck.

"What did he say?" she asks. "If the prime minister of Italy said anything like that, he'd be laughed off the stage. You talk about God and you'd never get elected to anything. You talk about what you're going to do about taxes, and then you shut up."

God bless the Republic of Italy, I say.

It's not the differences in our backgrounds that most fascinate me. It's the inconsistencies and the seeming contradictions. The distances between reputations and realities. Somewhat later in our relationship I was startled by a comment Elisa made at a high-end Italian design store in Manhattan. We were admiring various items, from cocktail mixing sets, to serving bowls, to lamps and furniture. When we came upon the ironing boards Elisa's eyes grew wide and sparkled in a way I'd thought only I was capable of causing. She admired the heavy-duty, beautifully designed contraptions and said, "If you ever want to buy me something, you could buy me this."

I was taken aback. I grew up with a mother who'd gone back to college and gotten a master's degree in the late 1960s, before the "women's movement" had made such endeavors mainstream. Back when the local bank manager wouldn't allow her to open an account *without her husband's signature and permission.* In my household there was a lot of talk about how "disgraceful," "inappropriate," and "disrespectful" it was to give a woman a gift whose purpose was to perform household chores. An iron? Ironing board? Vacuum cleaner? You'd be killed. Worse than killed; you'd live in torment the rest of your days.

The woman who'd already agreed to be my wife was saying she'd *like* an ironing board for her birthday. Not just any ironing board. A $350 ironing board. An ironing board that resembled scaffolding for a major construction site. Elisa is not a homemaker with no life outside of pleasing her husband through housework. She's a medical researcher who goes to a laboratory every day to investigate how the parathyroid hormone affects osteoblastic gene expression. She's not an American cliché. She is, though, an Italian cliché. (Not the osteoblastic gene expression part. That's not a cliché of any kind.) She's an Italian cliché in that she will not leave the house with un-ironed clothes. It's not done. You don't have anyone over to dinner without an ironed tablecloth. You don't even go to bed without ironed sheets. Consider all the differences between us: nationality, language, religion, culture, upbringing. It's the enthusiasm for ironing that sets us apart. That, and my dirty ass.

My wife claims she loves to iron, though I suspect it's the result she loves, not the activity. But I did not give her the ironing board for her birthday. Even if Elisa would be perfectly pleased with the gift, I'll never give it out of fear of what my mother might do to me.

The only circumstance that could alter my position would be if, by some miracle, Elisa and I could afford a house of our own. I don't mean to plead poverty; there are plenty of places in the world where we could afford to have a home of grand proportions. They just don't happen to be in an area where I can be employed on a network television show or where Elisa can work on a Fourier transform infrared imaging spectrometer. So we're stuck.

But if there were to be a house somewhere in our future, I'd give Elisa the gift she craves. The one that might make her feel at home in this strange and anything-but-superior land. It wouldn't be the house itself. But, buried in one of its smaller rooms, wrapped in colorful paper and decorated with ribbons, would be her first American bidet. Better yet, dueling "his and hers" models. Better still, one in every bathroom of the house, in case her mother or father come to visit. Maybe we'd put one on the front porch, to make sure no one enters without being fresh as a daisy. Forget wiping your feet, wash your ass before you come in!

There we'd be, the most sanitized, well-ironed family on the block. Now, if only we could get those delis and grocery stores to clean themselves up. Or even a fraction of the population to stop, clear their heads of the propaganda they've been force-fed since birth, to resist the urge to berate others while aggrandizing themselves, and to sit down and carefully, tenderly, with or without a washcloth or premoistened baby wipe (or even any prosciutto), make sure their own asses are as clean as they think they are, or as clean as they might be.

How Did You Two Meet?

I just knew. Like in all the fairy tales I'd never believed, like with all the couples whose stories I couldn't stand to hear. I saw the smile of the woman who'd later be my wife, felt an instant level of comfort and ease I'd never experienced before, and knew that I wanted to spend the rest of my life with her. I just knew.

The third time we met.

But, still . . .

"So, how did you two meet?"

It's the most common question asked of anyone who participates as one-half of a couple. Job interview, dinner party, high school reunion, adulterous liaison. Regardless of the surroundings (or even whether both parties are present), when the spouse comes up, the question inevitably follows. Of course, the terror of every inquisitor, and the bane of every event where the question is asked, are the people who think they've got a good story when they really don't. I think Elisa and I do.

Then again, I could be wrong.

OUR PAIRING SEEMS to amuse a lot of people. They express surprise that we were able to find each other. I'm known for my work as an actor. My wife makes a living performing infrared spectroscopic characterization of bone mineral and matrix properties of transgenic mice over-expressing insulin-like growth factor binding protein 5 (that's IGFBP-5, for those of you in the know). It's not the usual combination of careers.

My wife is a scientist. She earned a master's degree in pharmaceutical chemistry at the University of Bologna in the mid-1990s, then accepted a Rotary scholarship shortly afterward to come to the United States and earn a second master's degree in biophysical chemistry at Rutgers University in Newark, New Jersey. Bologna to Newark. That's moving up in the world. Besides the aesthetic compromises involved, the complicating factor of the two degrees was that while the first was studied for and accomplished in Italian, the second was taught, and earned, in English.

Me, I recite dialogue in front of a motion picture camera. The only scientific, or simply mathematical, thing I can say about my work is that the camera records it at twenty-four frames per second. Unless it's shooting video. Then I'm not sure what's going on.

So, how *did* we meet? Why did we seek each other out, over months and months, and fall in love? And how did I morph from a classic specimen of the man who can't commit, into a man who was sure he'd found exactly what he'd always wanted, and who went after it with less ambivalence than he'd ever felt about anything before? It's a good story. I think.

. . .

ON JUNE 1, 2002, my brother, Lowell, had a party at his new home in Rhinecliff, New York. The guests that day ranged from childhood friends to recent acquaintances. A number of them were people I'd spent hours with every day twenty to thirty years before, but had hardly seen or spoken with in the past ten. Images of those old friends were etched indelibly into my memory, but they'd since slimmed down or spread out, opened up or closed off, and been altered in other, less easily categorized ways. Core connections remained, but layers and layers of stranger had accumulated to cover up that core. Often, the stranger they'd come to resemble most was one of their parents. In the midst of these reunions I was introduced to a friend of my brother's named Jennifer. Jennifer introduced me to a friend she'd brought along named Elisa.

THE HUDSON RIVER Valley in New York State is one of the most beautiful regions in the world. It can also be, during the late spring to early autumn months, ridiculously hot, humid, and oppressively uncomfortable. By late morning, at my brother's gathering, the temperature was already approaching eighty-five degrees with the humidity hovering around sixty percent.

I was surprised by the way the exotically accented woman I'd just been introduced to was dressed. Elisa was wearing a black skirt, black fishnet stockings, and red high-heeled shoes. I thought she was ultrasophisticated and way out of my league.

Most of my relationships had been with small women, extremely slender, who tended to look years younger than they actually were. They were actresses, for the most part, or women who wanted to be actresses, and I tended to go for the ones who were intelligent and sexy, and who looked—give or take a few years—like they could have been teenagers.

Elisa would never be mistaken for anything other than a woman. She is, by any standards other than the anorexic ones of Hollywood, slim herself. But she's not a waif. Her curves weren't hidden by what she was wearing that day.

We spoke at my brother's party, but not more than a few sentences. The only exchange I recall was when I said, "Fantastic stockings."

SOME WEEKS LATER, at home in Santa Monica, I got a call from my brother's friend Jennifer telling me she and Elisa were in Napa Valley and that they'd soon be passing through Los Angeles. I wasn't surprised to hear from her. Jennifer had taken my number at my brother's house and told me she and Elisa would be traveling in California and that she'd get in touch. But the call was made from Elisa's cell phone. "Atti, E." showed up on my caller ID. I didn't delete the number from the phone's memory over the next few days, even though I already had Jennifer's number should I need it. Jennifer and I made plans for the three of us to get together about a week later.

I got a slightly better sense of Elisa during one evening out with her and Jennifer once they arrived in Santa Monica. Late that night, after we'd had dinner, they came back to my apartment for a drink. Elisa mimed slipping off the attractive-but-ill-designed chairs I'd purchased at a street fair.

I remember thinking, Oh, look at that. She's a clown.

Our senses of humor didn't mesh completely. Earlier in the evening, after passing a statue that overlooks the Pacific Ocean of the actual Santa Monica, I pulled out my tired L.A. joke that she was "the patron Saint of Screenplays."

Elisa nodded seriously.

"I'm kidding," I told her, not understanding how she could have misunderstood. But I was the one who didn't get it. I had no idea then that there are Catholic saints devoted to matters far more mundane than screenplay writing. There are patron saints of cooks and computer users. There are patron saints of librarians and lost articles. There is a patron saint against oversleeping.

A few weeks later I learned I'd be traveling to New York for a two-week trip for filming. I grabbed my phone and flipped through the saved numbers. "Atti, E." was there, right where I'd left it. I decided to give her a call.

But what was the protocol? I wondered. Elisa hadn't given me her phone number. She'd never even called me herself. I had the number only as a result of her friend's borrowing her cell phone to call me several weeks earlier. I couldn't decide whether calling her out of the blue would seem strange or simply be the adult thing to do (the key word there being "adult," and the key point being my unfamiliarity, at age forty, with what type of behavior constitutes it).

SEVERAL MONTHS BEFORE meeting Jennifer and Elisa I'd discovered Internet dating. I'd scanned a few websites and packed my schedule with meetings with complete strangers. This activity proved two contradictory facts: (1) there are large numbers of women I am capable of feeling attracted to, and (2) I feel compatibility with almost none of them. Internet dating is great. It's fascinating. It can even be fun. But it's also fucking exhausting.

One of the women I met was named Noelle. Noelle's "profile" had specified that she was interested in finding someone to date for a serious relationship, and that she wasn't interested in what's often categorized as "casual sex," "NSA" (no strings attached; c'mon, get with it), or "hookups," as the sites aimed at younger players call them. When I felt certain, by visit number three, that I wasn't interested in Noelle as a serious partner, I took her up on her encouragement to speak honestly. "After all," Noelle had said, "you've got friends and

I've got friends. If we don't hit it off with each other, maybe we'd like someone else one of us knows."

What a plan, I thought. Secondary benefits to less-than-ideal Internet dates endured. With little invested, each date (with an agreeable, open-minded collaborator) could exponentially expand your universe of potential dating partners.

But when I told Noelle that I didn't think a serious relationship between the two of us was going to interest me, her response was to lay one very serious kiss on me. She then suggested that there were other ways we could have fun. The mixed messages were flying around the room. They were screeching like banshees and bouncing off the walls.

In one of my better exercises of judgment, I resisted temptation. Noelle eased off her erotic enticement, expressed her understanding and agreement, and we vowed to remain friends. The one kiss, initiated by her, was the only vaguely sexual event to pass between us. About a week later I was asked to join Noelle and some of her friends for a dinner party. I found myself immediately attracted to, and bantering playfully with, a friend of hers named Lynne. I thought the Internet dating dividends might be about to pay off. The next day I spent ten seconds locating Lynne's name in the phone book and gave her a call. She was glad to hear from me, and we set up a date.

Those of you who are a lot smarter than I am—or simply in possession of better instincts—should be having a good laugh already. For those who need to have it explained, I'd walked myself into an ambush. I was about to get hammered from both sides.

The first call came from Lynne.

"How did you get my number?" she demanded.

"I looked your name up in the phone book."

That seemed to take her by surprise.

"Well, I thought you'd gotten it from Noelle. I just called her to tell her we were going out, and she's really upset."

"Why?" I asked. "Noelle and I both agreed we weren't interested in being involved with each other. She's the one who offered to introduce me to her friends."

"Well, I think you'd better call her," Lynne said. "I wouldn't be comfortable going out with you until you cleared things up with her."

I didn't get the chance to call, because the phone rang again and this time it was Noelle.

"I can't believe you called Lynne without telling me first."

"But, Noelle, you offered to introduce me to your friends. You *did* introduce me to one of them. All I did was call her up."

"Well, it was disrespectful of you to ask her out without telling me first."

So my confusion about what constitutes "adult behavior" (or what the rules are in regard to phone numbers caught by caller ID off cell phones borrowed from friends) might now be more understandable. The definition of "adult" seems to vary from group to group, and from circumstance to circumstance. It's plastic, so to speak.

I had only one date with Lynne, who turned out to still be in love with the boyfriend she'd stopped seeing two weeks earlier. We took a hike in a park above the Pacific Ocean where she told me how gorgeous his cock was, and how he'd seduced her into enjoying anal sex even though she'd previously been sure she had no interest in it. I'm not against discussing beautiful cocks and anal sex on first dates. I just happen to prefer that the sex and the cock under discussion have some potential of involving me, or mine.

As we rounded a bend in the middle of the woods, Lynne stopped short and gasped. I thought there must have been a rattlesnake in our path and jumped back. Barely in view in the distance was a young couple lying on a blanket just off to the side of the trail. They were deeply entwined, as close to having sex as two fully clothed people could be.

"I think that's my boyfriend!" Lynne hissed. "He told me he was at work today." She whipped out her cell phone in the middle of the woods and started to dial.

What am I doing here? I thought. This is what I got yelled at by two people to enjoy? A woman suffering from anal sex withdrawal, watching her supposedly ex-boyfriend—whom she still speaks with every day—humping some other woman in the woods? If we'd been anywhere near civilization I would have been tempted to just walk away. Since we were in the wilderness the only place I could have walked, other than straight ahead toward the couple on the trail, was off a cliff.

Lynne got no answer at her ex-boyfriend's office. She spent a long time staring ahead, then examining the trail behind. She looked as if she were considering the possibility of backtracking and redoing the two-mile loop we'd already nearly completed. Finally she smiled and said, "It's okay. I don't think it's him." She walked past the couple, and away from me.

Internet dating. Lots of fun. Very tiring.

PERHAPS IT'S NOW more clear why I was less than sure how to proceed when it came to calling Elisa. I even considered calling her friend Jennifer to pretend I needed to ask for Elisa's phone number even though I already had it. Thank goodness I finally decided to act like a grown-up, which to me meant picking up the phone and just giving a call.

"Hi, Elisa. This is Evan Handler calling. I'm the guy you and Jennifer had dinner with a few weeks ago in Santa Monica. I'm going to be in New York for a couple of weeks starting Monday, and I wondered if you might like to get together while I'm in town."

I left my phone number, spent two weeks in New York, and didn't hear a word.

Ouch, I thought. Okay. Not interested.

Three weeks later, when I was back in Santa Monica, Elisa called. She'd been in Italy visiting her family and had just gotten my message.

I was thrilled by her enthusiasm, since it meant I hadn't been rejected. I was, unfortunately, not as thrilled by her apparent availability. The new wrinkle was that, over the two weeks in New York, while hearing nothing from Elisa, I'd allowed my Australian infatuation to rebloom. Out of frustration with the dearth of enticing partners we were meeting, Abbey Leigh and I had both taken to overlooking the violent disagreements we'd had while living together in Los Angeles eighteen months earlier. When I told the women at *Sex and the City* I was considering going to Sydney to surprise my understandably guarded (and presumably still-tempestuous) ex, they had a grand time in the makeup trailer referencing one of their earlier episodes.

"Evan's making the Big Gesture!" they shouted to each other. "Evan's going to make the Big Gesture!" Somehow, with the endorsement of a past plotline of a hit show, as well as the enthusiasm of its female stars, flying myself unannounced to Sydney, Australia, to see the woman I'd fallen in love with two years earlier while engaged to someone else, but whom I didn't sleep with or have a real relationship with until a year after that, and whom I hadn't seen for a year and a half since, didn't seem like such a lamebrained idea. I'm embarrassed to admit it now, but I didn't exactly light up at Elisa's call.

"I don't expect to be in New York again for the next six months," I told her. And it was the truth. But when Elisa tells the story, this is the part where she says she told her friend Jennifer she'd never call me again.

Human beings will often take turns doing to others whatever might have most recently been done to them. I got my comeuppance from Abbey Leigh as if she were getting back at me not only for rejecting her but for everything I'd ever done to all the other women I've been involved with. I flew myself to Sydney and surprised her, and got a warm welcome. She was touched by the gesture, and we spent six romantic days together. We said good-bye, and said we'd be in touch to talk and discuss. Then she didn't respond to any of my e-mails or phone messages for two months.

Back on native soil, I got an unexpected invitation to spend a weekend in New York visiting a *Sex and the City* colleague. She and I barely knew each other, but had spent one night together after the previous season's wrap party. Since she also happened to live in a one-room apartment, the understanding was I'd stay in a hotel and we'd play the visit out by ear. As a single man in my forties, these were the possibilities I'd become accustomed to pursuing.

I can't really say I had high hopes that my work colleague and I would form a lasting connection, but I didn't know her well enough to be sure. I flew back across the continent just to keep open the avenues of investigation. Of course, I was still the kind of guy who preferred having more than one avenue to investigate at a time, so I also called Elisa Atti to let her know I was coming back to town.

Elisa and I made plans to get together for a walk in Central Park. From the instant she walked into the lobby of the Royalton Hotel where I was staying, I was smitten in a way I hadn't previously been. Elisa's smile, spirit, and enthusiasm sizzled in the cooler-than-cool hotel lobby, and I felt just as much heat blasting off her once we'd stepped out into the warmth of the day. We talked about her work and our lives, we laughed at ourselves and each other and everyone we saw on the street. Since I'd spoken the word "Frappuccino," we went hunting for a Starbucks before heading into the park. Elisa felt she needed to experience whatever kind of bastardized Italo-American concoction that might prove to be.

We sat enraptured with each other on a park bench for two hours. We talked about families, jobs, and Elisa's uncertainty over what English words were appropriate to speak during sex. What I most recall is that, in spite of no overlapping experiences or shared background, we seemed in nearly complete agreement on every issue, similarly inclined toward lifestyle choices, and like-minded in terms of taste. I also found her to be a more fully mature, self-sufficient person than any of the American women I'd known. Elisa was deeply engrossed in her scientific research, yet her interests outside of work ran toward the artistic, especially dance, cinema, and cuisine. In opposition to most of the entertainment industry friends I had, Elisa seemed happy with her position in her field. I kept thinking to myself, My God, this is exactly the kind of woman I've wished I could find my whole life.

Elisa and I had arranged our get-together in the most low-key, low-expectation, two-people-just-getting-to-know-each-other way. Since our afternoon together hadn't been defined as a "date," we also asked each other whether we were currently involved in relationships. I told Elisa I'd come to town to spend some time with someone I didn't really yet know, and my heart sank when she told me she'd been dating a photographer.

"But I don't think I'm going to marry him," she said.

I wasn't listening anymore. I was only wondering how to win over the woman I'd just met, whom I was crazy about already, but who'd just told me she was involved with someone else. When it was time for Elisa to meet Jennifer for a movie, I wandered off with no idea what, if anything, our meeting had meant to her. I'd made a ham-fisted bid for another get-together when she told me she was traveling to New Jersey the next day to have her hair cut.

"Well, then I'll have to see you on Sunday before I fly back to Los Angeles. So I can tell you how it looks."

Elisa just laughed, and walked away.

I went back to my hotel, phoned the woman I'd flown to New York to see, and told her I needed to call off whatever it was we had going on. I made a series of additional calls to friends, asking them how to most respectfully (and most successfully) pursue a woman who's already got a boyfriend. My ex Liz, the *Sex and the City* writer, said,

"That's a tough one." My *Sex and the City* costar Dave broadcast his advice like a ringside announcer.

"Fight for her!" he said. Which I had no idea how to do.

ELISA AND I spoke the next night. She called in frustration after trying to watch a defective tape of *Sex and the City*, a show she'd never seen. She again mentioned her plans for Sunday, which now included a Circle Line Sightseeing Cruise around Manhattan Island. Her parents, who'd never been to the United States, were coming for a visit in less than a week and Elisa wanted to see whether it would be something she thought they'd enjoy.

"I've never ridden the Circle Line, either," I said. Then, before she could fend off my imposition, I repeated my desire to see her new haircut. Elisa laughed and agreed to meet me on Sunday to ride the boat around Manhattan together.

OUR AFTERNOON ON the rivers felt as special as our afternoon in Central Park. We didn't do anything other than what people falling in love in New York usually do. We ogled the city's skyline, and mocked the annoying banter of the overly amplified tour guide. We speculated on the personalities of the tourists around us, and we traveled closer to the Statue of Liberty than we'd ever been. The most surprising aspect of the afternoon was that alongside my fascination I felt *familiarity*.

That's an odd juxtaposition for a second meeting with a woman from another world. But all I wanted to do was pair up with Elisa. Because I *loved* her. Not in a crazy way. Not in the way of a deep attachment, earned over time. Just as in a superlative adequate to communicate the level of enjoyment I got from proximity to her spirit. I "loved" her because "like" wasn't a strong enough word to convey the level of my pleasure in her presence. I loved the two afternoons I'd spent with her. I loved the conversations I'd had with her. I loved everything I'd discovered about her. I loved her simply for *being* her. That's what my ex-fiancée Patricia had complained was missing in our relationship. Now that I'd tasted it, I couldn't blame her for insisting upon it.

When it was time for us to part on Sixth Avenue near Houston Street I felt I couldn't let the opportunity slip away. I was scheduled to fly back to Los Angeles early the next morning. I decided to go with my friend Dave's advice and take a swing.

"Look," I said. "I'm not in the habit of pursuing women who already have boyfriends. But I like you more than I've ever liked anyone before. If there was ever a time when you *weren't* seeing someone, if you wanted me to, I'd be willing to come back to New York just so I could spend some more time with you."

Elisa took the first sentence well. She brightened as I assured her I didn't chase other men's girlfriends. But when I spoke the words "I like you more than I've ever liked anyone before," her face blanched. It wasn't a subtle occurrence. And she didn't reciprocate. I believe the one word she spoke was, "Okay."

I walked away not sure which of two things had gone wrong. Either I'd miscalculated her feelings, and I'd been the only one swimming in delirium over the past two days; or I'd miscommunicated what I'd meant to say to someone who didn't speak English as her first language. As soon as I was back in my hotel room I ripped open my laptop and put together an e-mail.

"Elisa," I wrote. "I want to make a clarification. When I said I like you better than anyone I've ever met, I meant I've felt a stronger sense of attraction, and a stronger sense of being around someone who possesses the qualities I've wanted to be around, than I have before. I'm aware we barely know each other. I meant to say something strong, but I didn't mean to say anything insane. "

Then, thinking it was witty (and forgetting, again, that we didn't share firm lingual common ground), I added, "So I'd like to take this opportunity to assure you that there are many women I've known for many years, who I'm close to already, who I like much more than you." And I signed my name.

Elisa didn't catch my tongue-in-cheek intent. I have to admit, my execution wasn't ideal. My advice to those wooing women whose first languages don't match their own is that, generally speaking, tongue-in-cheekiness doesn't translate.

In spite of the misunderstanding, Elisa e-mailed me two days later to let me know she'd broken off her relationship and was no longer seeing anyone. I made plans to travel back to New York.

ELISA AND I had our first "official" date four months after I complimented her stockings. When I dropped her off outside the subway on Fifth Avenue we kissed tentatively. It was the only night of my visit we didn't spend together. And it was the last day I didn't call Elisa my girlfriend, or something more.

We spent the rest of my ten-day stay seeing movies at the New York Film Festival, watching Al Pacino play Arturo Ui, eating out, and staying up until three, four, and five A.M. talking and making love. On the fifth day, immediately after Elisa had left our hotel suite to go to work, I knelt down on the carpet and gave thanks to God for allowing me to find her. I supposed, as I did it, I might have to reevaluate whether or not I believed in the entity I was giving thanks to. For the time being I was too happy to examine anything. I didn't care what I believed. I just knew I had found what I wanted, and what I'd come to believe wasn't ever going to be mine.

ELISA AND I share a similar way of walking through the world. It's as simple as that. We have an innate understanding of the other's point of view. I suppose it comes down to respect. It's not that I didn't have it for the other women I've been with, only that I didn't realize how much deeper and more complete it could be.

THAT'S OUR STORY. I'm not sure it's radically different from millions of others'. Two people meet, feel an unprecedented level of attraction and affection for each other, discover their intuitions are correct, and fall madly in love (oh, and question everything they believe about life, love, relationships, and God along the way). But I'm also aware there are countless other millions who've not had the good fortune of finding a mate who gives them the depth of pleasure I've described. Not everyone does. I know, because for a couple of decades I was one of them.

But that's just where the story begins, isn't it? As comparable as the similarities in all relationships are, the divergences eventually multiply exponentially. But that's not the question that was posed. It wasn't "Where did you go from there?" or "How are you guys doing today?" It was "How did you two meet?"

My wife, Elisa, and I have a good answer. Of course, the terror of every inquisitor, and the bane of every event where the question is asked, are the people who think they've got a good story when they really don't. I think Elisa and I do.

A Little **Fame and** Lots of **Women**

HERE'S A CONFESSION sure to make me unpopular: I got married not long ago, but I'm already finding it difficult to remain faithful. I haven't abandoned the idea. It's just proving a challenge.

I'm not very famous. The vast majority of Americans—hell, the vast majority of television viewers—would not know me by name. "Semi-recognizable" is about as high as my status rises. Nevertheless, as a result of a series of appearances on a few popular television programs, a wide assortment of people are now excited to meet me. Many of these people are women—the same women who would have turned away from me in disgust had I dared to engage them in conversation prior to my image being broadcast into their homes. Now they seek me out. They become shy and deferential in my presence.

One might think, being aware of these facts, I'd be less than enthused by their attention. The truth is the opposite. I find it thoroughly enjoyable.

. . .

MY POPULARITY EMERGED out of the ether on the night I went on my first date with Elisa. We walked twenty-five blocks to get to the theater where we were to see the Broadway production of *Frankie and Johnny in the Claire de Lune* starring Stanley Tucci and Edie Falco. The twist was that, since our first tentative meeting in Central Park a month earlier, my character on *Sex and the City* had made several additional appearances. As Elisa and I tried to make our way through Times Square to the theater, fans of the show started to besiege me with requests for photos and autographs. Those not within reach were calling out from all directions.

"Harry!" people were screaming. "Look! Look! It's Harry! Hi, Harry!" This had never happened to me before.

I wondered whether or not we were going to make it to the theater on time. I wondered whether I was going to be forced to cultivate a reputation for being rude to my fans on my very first day of being famous in *order* to get to the theater on time. I also wondered whether my date thought this was what my life had been like on any day before this one. Finally, in spite of how smitten I was by Elisa, I wondered whether the moment when sexy young women were shouting to me was the best time to meet the person with whom I thought I might be able to really make a go of it. The first three musings answered themselves promptly and without significant incident. Number four required some more intensive introspection (not to mention self-restraint), and would come to symbolize the ironic theme of the next phase of my life.

Suddenly, on nights I'd find myself out unaccompanied by my wife, young women would initiate the most intimate conversations. These were women whose fathers could have been my age. That didn't stop them from telling me about their sexual exploits, as well as those of their girlfriends. It didn't stop them from telling me about the sexual exploits they'd had *with* their girlfriends.

"But you're famous," one twenty-two-year-old told me. "I'm sure you know how to find two girls who'd like to be with you together whenever you want."

Apparently my life, to this point, has been misspent because I know no such thing.

I've LEARNED HOW to deal with the situation. I've learned how to avoid not only infidelity but also any feelings of frustration in letting women pass me by. The solution to the problem is the opposite of what I'd thought it was before meeting my wife. Previously, I'd thought the answer was to avoid spending time with anyone I found myself attracted to. I've since learned that the answer is actually the opposite. Spend time with them. Talk to them. Almost invariably the results are that the women turn out to be people I wouldn't want to alter my life for. Often it turns out they're not people I'd even want to have a very long conversation with.

Problems arise with the exceptions to this rule. In those cases it's best not only to turn and run but to do or say something unforgivable before doing so. Something simple. Like letting a woman know I already have a wife, whom I love.

But it's been a less common issue than I thought it would be. Because another thing I've noticed about the fickle creatures now drawn my way is that their interest in me is fleeting. No matter how thrilled they might be to have spotted me, or to get to photograph or to speak with me, it's only a matter of minutes before the pheromones send everyone back where they belong. Apparently, the place these young women belong is back with the taller guys.

I owe MY minor celebrity status to the circuitous casting of the role of Harry Goldenblatt (Charlotte's divorce-lawyer-turned-husband) on the HBO television show *Sex and the City*. After twenty-six consecutive years of living in Manhattan, I moved myself and my belongings to Santa Monica, California. Within days of my furniture arriving I got a call from a close friend who'd been newly hired as a staff writer for the show. She also happened to be an ex-girlfriend, but pretty much everyone who's lived in Manhattan and worked in the entertainment industry for as long as I have is everyone else's ex-something-or-other.

My ex-girlfriend told me she'd overheard a conversation between Sarah Jessica Parker and Cynthia Nixon, both of whom I'd known slightly over the years, in which they'd both agreed I would be a great choice for a new role being written into the show. I hung up the phone from that conversation very excited.

Then I heard about the casting breakdown being prepared for release to the talent agents in New York and Los Angeles. Harry Goldenblatt, the character who would be introduced as a love interest for the extremely particular Charlotte York, played by the ravishing Kristin Davis, was being described as "boorish, overbearing, and unattractive."

"I never would have thought to recommend you," my ex-girlfriend the writer assured me. "I didn't think you were right for it." Maybe she was trying to be kind. If so, the attempt was undercut when she told me she'd been pushing another actor for the role for weeks already.

Thus was established the egotistical existential dilemma that would define the next two years of my life. My actor ego and my personal vanity started to do battle and I wondered at which indignity (contained within this fantastic opportunity) I should take greater offense: that my ex-girlfriend had doubted my ability to outwit any other actors in playing any role at all, or the fact that Sarah Jessica Parker and Cynthia Nixon both thought me a suitable choice to play the ugly guy.

. . .

ONCE I WAS hired, the story lines over the first few episodes concerned Charlotte's repulsion over Harry's looks, his sweating proclivi-
ties, his table manners, his excessively hairy back, *and* the subsequent
rash that resulted from his agreeing to have it waxed. They were all
given prominent screen exposure. That was before my naked ass
was given prominent exposure in an episode about Harry's tendency
to sit on white upholstered furniture without any clothes on. My sole
comfort at this point (other than the fact that I was working with great
people on a truly funny hit show, of course) was that each script
mentioned that Harry was the best lover Charlotte had ever had.

If it seems I'd gotten way too caught up in the confusion between a
fictional character and me and my own behavior, don't worry. These
thoughts didn't consume me. Though they were hard to ignore. When
I walked down the street people would yell, "Hey, look, it's the hairy-
back guy!" When I was introduced to a woman, she'd say, "I can't
believe I'm just meeting you and I've already seen your ass." A companion would often whisper, in mock conspiratorial fashion, "Yeah,
and he's supposed to be really good in bed."

It was hard to ignore the judgments and comparisons, since they
were also being talked about in the press, which was brand-new to
me. On *Regis and Kelly*, on *The View*, and on *Late Night with Conan
O'Brien*. They all wanted me to comment on an article that had
appeared in the New York *Daily News* around the time of my first
appearance on the show. The article was about the men of *Sex and the
City*, and it featured a small photograph of each of us. The newspaper
claimed to have asked a panel of fifteen young women to rate the characters—the characters, mind you, not the men who played them—in
terms of which one they'd most like to take to bed.

The good news is I didn't come in last. I didn't come in next-to-
last, either. But I did come in sixth out of eight, finishing ahead of

only Charlotte's first husband, Trey, who couldn't maintain an erection, and Samantha's ex, Richard, whom she'd walked in on while his head was buried between the legs of another woman. So I did beat out two characters, but they were the characters who, according to the story lines, represented impotence and infidelity.

Over the course of the next year, perceptions about my character started to change. Most articles and news stories still referred to me as being something other than traditionally attractive. But they also started referring to me, amazingly enough, as a sex symbol. The term was always preceded by the word "unlikely," though. "Unlikely" sex symbol. Still, compared with that *Daily News* article, I felt progress was being made. Now, when I made my way around New York, I got a constant stream of backhanded compliments.

"Did you lose *weight*?" I'd be asked. "You look so much *fatter* on the show. Look at him, Bill. He looks so much *fatter* on the show."

Interesting to me was the fact that Bill, or Sam, or Simon, or whoever the husband happened to be, never responded. I don't know if that was because they sympathized with me, or just didn't give a damn about me, or the show, at all.

But men do watch the show. I know this because they started to approach me, too. And here's where—though I'm a little sensitive about applying a cultural stereotype—a Semitic emphasis creeps in. I'd guess a solid seventy-five percent of the men who've stopped me to comment on the show have been Jewish.

"*Thank you* for what you're doing on that show," I've been told, over and over. "*Thank you.*"

I don't know whether most of the thanks were offered because they thought it was a positive portrayal of a Jewish character, or if they were thrilled I'd defiled television's ultimate rendition of another cultural stereotype: the shiksa goddess. I say I'm not sure about *most* of the thanks because many of the men made it perfectly clear which aspect of the program they took the most pleasure in. On more than one occasion I've been told, "You give it to her *good*!"

.   .   .

A LOT OF times I get asked about the similarities between me and the character of Harry Goldenblatt, or of the similarities between the four actresses and the characters they played. I'm sorry if it disappoints, but beyond saying that I'm genuinely fond of each of them, I don't say anything about those ladies in public or in print. Because it's treacherous.

I went on *Regis and Kelly* early on to help promote the show. I was asked how my new wife felt about the sex scenes I'd filmed with Kristin Davis. I said she was being a good sport about it. And she was. Then I added that she had a habit of calling me in my dressing room at the studio and saying, jokingly, in her lovely Italian accent, "Are you kissing that slut? Are you kissing her?"

It was all in good fun, and it got a good laugh. But it turned out Kristin Davis wasn't so happy. I was told that if I go on television and tell a story where my wife refers to her as a slut, even jokingly, it was my responsibility to say, "But Kristin Davis isn't a slut at all. She's a lovely woman, and a hardworking actress."

So since I've told the story again: "Kristin Davis isn't a slut at all. She's a lovely woman, and a hardworking actress."

I hope that takes care of that.

THE QUESTION I get asked most now is how it *feels* to be famous. The most accurate description is one I rarely give, because it comes across as self-aggrandizing. But it feels like I've become a National Landmark, and that I have Superpowers.

I say National Landmark because people now stop and stare, or pull over and photograph, just the way they do when they get a glimpse of the Statue of Liberty or the Empire State Building. They point and call out to one another, as if I'm not human and can't hear. "Look . . . look! Quick! Turn around! It's the guy from *Sex and the City*!" And that happens everywhere I walk, wherever I go. It depends, of course, on the recognition factor that day—variables that range from the city or nation I'm in, to the demographics of the crowd, to even the temperature and barometric pressure. Sometimes I'm completely invisible, while other times it's like being a boat skimming across the water, leaving a wake of pointing people behind.

The best aspect is perhaps the strangest. These glimpses make people *happy*. I mean, it makes them really, *really* happy. Just to have seen me. I offer these people nothing (other than politeness should they want to say hello or snap a photo). Yet, the mere fact of my appearance excites them and improves their mood. If you can imagine what it would feel like to walk around in a city where you don't know anyone and have dozens of strangers light up and become happier than they were the moment before just for having glimpsed you, then you should understand why I say it's like having Superpowers. I can't leap tall buildings in a single bound, but I'm not sure what other term to use to describe the phenomenon.

My surge in popularity came late, at forty-two. It was also abrupt, like a light switch being flipped. One second it was off, the next it was on. I'm aware of how randomly selected I was for it. I'm aware how unrelated it is to anything about *me* (other than that I happened to portray a character in a popular television show). Had I been younger, I would have thought I'd earned it. I'd have thought I was getting my due (actually, when I was younger I *did* think it was my due, I just felt it was being unjustly withheld). Now I enjoy it for the novelty it is.

ON DAYS WHEN I'm neither invisible nor creating commotion, when my recognition quotient resides at an in-between level, I get the second most commonly asked question.

"Do I know you from somewhere?"

It's an odd inquiry, in that it presupposes that I know more about the information stored inside the inquisitor's brain than he or she does. And it's tough to answer. What I've learned to do is answer honestly, but without complete candor.

"I don't know," I'll say. "My name is Evan." And I offer my hand.

I'm fairly certain these people know me from seeing me on film or in a television show. But offering up this possibility is always a mistake. I know, because I used to try.

"Oh. What would I have seen you in?" they ask.

And here's where we come to the action to be most assiduously avoided: the recitation of the résumé. I have never provided a successful recitation of the résumé. Each attempt has led my examiner to declare, as I cycle through title after title, with mounting pride in each monosyllabic response, "No . . . No . . . No . . . *No* . . . *No* . . . *NO* . . . *NO* . . ." Even if I'm right, it's best not to go there.

A lot of people don't ask whether or not they know me. They *tell* me they do. And they tell me from where.

"Hey, I know you from CBI. You worked in the cubicle next to me."

And then it's my turn to say "No."

"Greyhound, right?"

"No."

"Hey . . . ! Hunter High."

"No."

"You're friends with Ken and Sheila, right?"

"No."

"You used to skate with Uggy in the park."

"No."

"Yes, yes . . ."

"N—"

"Don't say no, you did!"

"No."

"*Yes.* Yes, you *did.* You used to skate with Uggy in the park!"

So, the recognition factor can have its less delightful moments. But for the most part (and I mean the 99.9 percent part), it's been a pure pleasure. I'm grateful to the people who have been so gracious toward me, and I'm grateful to the Fates that have bestowed the strange status upon me.

As A PRIVATE aside, without confirming or denying anything I've said so far: Uggy, I just got a rad new board. I'll meet you in the park Wednesday at noon.

Renovations and Terminations

TEN MONTHS AFTER the relief of leaving New York City for California, I moved myself, and all my belongings, back to Manhattan. I'd found every bit of the respite I'd sought in Santa Monica—from overcrowding, from congestion, from rude checkout clerks, bank tellers, and subway token booth attendants who seemed to hate me as much as they hated their jobs. But there were two irresistible lures drawing me back. One was a full year's employment filming the sixth and final season of *Sex and the City*. The other was Elisa.

The initial bliss of finding each other and falling in love had remained just that. But we'd continued to travel across the country at every opportunity in an attempt to get to know each other. The plan was to take things slow. I would be returning to New York two months before my work was scheduled to start to rehearse and perform a play in which I'd costar with Cynthia Nixon. The play was called *String Fever*, and it was a beautiful and wickedly funny meditation on the nature of existence as mused upon by a woman who's just passed forty and whose life and relationships are spinning out of control. Her ex-boyfriend, whom she still loves, has abandoned her and is spiraling into mental illness. Her father, hospitalized from a suicide attempt, is barely recovering from his own bouts with instability. Her best friend is dying of breast cancer. Another old friend, an Icelandic comedy star, is sending her semicoherent videotaped messages from his own odyssey of recurrent alcoholism as he travels the world searching for his wife, who's left him after one too many infidelities.

Meanwhile, the play's central character meets a string theorist who seduces her into not only an affair but also a flirtation with belief in a ten-dimensional, vibrating, unifying theory of all matter while she investigates methods of both natural and artificial insemination.

The play ends with the protagonist pregnant, soaking in the mineral springs of Iceland's fabled Blue Lagoon. Both the Icelandic comedian and her deteriorating, cancerous friend accompany her, and the three of them speculate on life's mysteries. Her relationships with both the physicist and the musician have ended, and her father has died. The sire of her child is unknown, though all three of the surviving male characters are revealed as possibilities.

As convoluted as it sounds, the plot and characters nearly mirror the experiences of the playwright, my old friend and ex-fiancée Jackie, who'd been my companion during my illness two decades earlier. The man she'd been with for ten years after we'd split had left her after plunging into drug addiction. Her father had attempted suicide by stabbing himself six times, surviving only due to scar tissue from earlier surgeries that had built up around his heart. Jackie's best friend had died horribly of cancer the year before at the age of forty-two. The only invention of the play was that Jackie hadn't gotten pregnant; she'd only dreamed about it.

But my new girlfriend, Elisa, did.

.   .   .

I WAS LIVING temporarily in an apartment on Forty-ninth Street, waiting for my New York home to have its wood floors refinished. A couple of weeks into the run of the play, Elisa—whom I'd been seeing only sporadically on a transcontinental basis for barely three months—started to feel strange.

Pregnancy seemed a ludicrous possibility. In spite of my sterility, we'd been mostly consistent in our use of contraceptives. But her symptoms persisted, so she tried a home pregnancy test. I was in the bedroom while she was in the bathroom. I wanted to give my new girlfriend some privacy, as well as attempt to reassure her through my casual behavior. My heart froze when I heard her voice, small and uncertain.

"Evan? Could you come here, please?"

I sped toward the bathroom, hoping she was simply confused by an inconclusive result. She handed the vial to me with hands that were shaking. Appearing to be in shock, she asked me to interpret what couldn't have been clearer. The test was positive. Elisa started to tremble, and collapsed sobbing into my arms. The Lord (or the strings, if you subscribe to the bridge between the general relativity and quantum theories) does work in mysterious ways.

THIS WAS NOT supposed to be within the realm of possibility. I'd had sperm counts done immediately after and several years post–bone marrow transplantation and was told that I had "severe fertility issues." This translated into the equivalent of what I was told was all but absolute sterility, with no chance of reversal. When I asked about statistical probabilities—a line of inquiry I'd generally avoided in regard to all aspects of illness—I was told the chances of conceiving a child through intercourse were "one in a million."

"But don't count on that," I was cautioned, lest I depend on past chemotherapy as adequate birth control. "It only takes one."

And I didn't. Not usually, anyway. A few times, here or there, I'd been less than vigilant. I somehow managed to defy odds even greater than those that had once lined up against my existence and achieved a successful conception, with a woman I barely knew, but with whom I already suspected I wanted to stay. It was, it seemed, a miracle. It was also a disaster.

HOLDING ELISA IN the bathroom was a surreal and terrifying experience. We'd become surprisingly attached in just three months, but there was no way to pretend we knew each other well. Each visit had been initiated by our confessing that, upon greeting each other at the airport, we'd had the sensation of embracing a stranger. It consistently took a day or two for us to refamiliarize ourselves with each other. And I'd never seen her so upset. I was shocked by the violence of her reaction. She was clearly terrified, and her terror had a profound effect on me. In a sudden, stabbing way that moment was reminiscent of when I'd been told my life was probably over nearly two decades earlier. Though the two occurrences were thematic opposites—one portending new life, the other prefacing its likely end—in both cases I learned that my desires were not what I had believed them to be a nanosecond before.

Before meeting Elisa I was the guy who, upon seeing a baby or a small child, would unabashedly proclaim, "Oh, I want to have a kid." As far as I knew, I'd meant it. It also got a hell of a reaction from any woman nearby, and I didn't mind that at all. Apparently there aren't so many single men pining aloud for parenthood.

For years, I'd had fantasies of what might happen if one of my girlfriends got pregnant. What if I had wanted to preserve the pregnancy while a girlfriend didn't? Because of its improbability, it would most likely be my only chance. The semen samples I'd stored in 1985, as well as those stored in 1988, were already older than the oldest I'd ever heard of being used for a successful conception. Those sperm were now high school aged. In spite of my secular tendencies it would have seemed a crime to extinguish such an unlikely potentiality. An unintended pregnancy had the possibility of becoming an explosive situation.

I'd imagined girlfriends becoming pregnant, I'd imagined their reluctance to go forward with the pregnancy, and I'd imagined myself begging them to reconsider. I'd imagined myself explaining to them the miracle that had occurred, and how, due to my reproductively challenged state, it must have been God's will (God's will?) that this child be brought into the world. I'd imagined scenarios whereby they relented, and those in which they refused. I'd imagined crushing emotional pain as we fought over the custody of children neither of us was prepared to care for, and over the loss of children they weren't willing to carry to term. I'd imagined it all so intensely, I believe, because it would have been one of the very worst things that could have happened. And because that's the kind of thing I do.

All those imaginings involved women I knew I wasn't destined to share my life with. Here I was, with a woman with whom I felt an unprecedented sense of compatibility, and the situation seemed even worse. With previous girlfriends, my desire to meet and love and raise our child *would not have posed a threat to the relationship itself.* It would have been easier to accept the responsibilities of parenthood with someone ill-suited as my long-term partner because, even if we were to split up, there wouldn't have been so much to lose. With Elisa, the formula was reversed. It felt as if everything was at stake. As it's turned out, nearly everything was.

Uptown on Eighty-ninth Street, a man named Moti had been hired to refinish the wood floors of my apartment. Elisa had been clear that even though we'd now be in the same city, she thought we should continue to live separately. She was just beginning her life as an independent adult before we'd met. She'd moved into her own studio apartment in Queens only a few months before, after years of living with roommates. She was brand-new in this country, and she was brand-new in her job. We both harbored trepidations about whether our feelings for each other would hold up if we lived together so soon. In the type of incongruity common to modern relationships, we both believed that maintaining a certain degree of distance and independence would be crucial to giving us the best chance at coming closer together. Instant parenthood didn't mesh with any of our definitions of "distance and independence."

Still, in the kind of contradictory choreography that's common to budding love, Elisa was helping me choose wood floor finishes and paint colors for the apartment. We intended to take things one step at a time. But the understanding was that we might, someday, be sharing that Manhattan co-op ("might" being the word that allowed all hopes and dreams to be fully expressed).

Moti was a character. He was an Israeli immigrant who told stories of his service in the Israeli army. We spent a fair amount of time together planning the apartment's renovations, and we spoke of New York City and the post-9/11 world. I expressed astonishment that buses hadn't yet started blowing up in Manhattan, as they do periodically in Jerusalem.

"It's going to happen," Moti answered. "It's coming here next. And when it does, then America will know." He said it in a way that made me think he both dreaded its arrival and might be responsible for it, whenever it came to pass.

Moti visited us on Forty-ninth Street, displaying samples of wood stains and complimenting our taste and our commitment to each other. He spoke of his own pregnant wife. Elisa and I glanced at each other each time Moti turned his back, silently acknowledging our secret.

"Leeesten to me," Moti said at the beginning of every sentence when we talked about the floor. Each expression of my own anxiety, every question designed to elicit some form of reassurance, brought forth a series of Moti's commands. "Leeesten to me," he'd say. "It's going to look beee-yeu-tee-ful. You're going to be very happy with it, Evan. You leeesten to me."

ELISA WAS WITH ME when I opened the door to my Eighty-ninth Street apartment. Moti and his team had finished their work the day before. At first glance it looked as if the floor had been painted with a thick coat of glossy white paint. Upon closer inspection—meaning by taking another quick look around—it became apparent that the floors were dreadfully scarred. There were deep grooves carved into the entire lengths and widths of every room. The floors of the living room, bedroom, and hallways now curved and sloped like a roller coaster. In several spots, the deepest grooves dug into the floor below the level where the tongues and grooves of each wood plank met—a possible deathblow that might cause the entire floor to buckle. My beautiful New York home looked like a gang of vandals had attacked it, working with knives and shovels instead of sandpaper. The job was a debacle, performed by an amateur.

"I can feeex it, Evan," Moti told me when I got him on the phone. "Leeesten to me. I can feeex it."

I told Moti not only that he'd not be continuing with any more work, but that I wanted back all the money I'd paid him so far.

"Evan, I'm making beeeuteeful floors now for twelve years. You're going to tell me how to make a beeeuteeful floor? Leeesten to me, you're going to be very happy. You leeesten to me."

But all he said when asked for an explanation was, "I made a meeestake."

THE FLOORS WERE eventually restored (but not without some degree of permanent damage) by a reputable company. Elisa and I then started working with samples of paint colors for the walls as we discussed the much more serious issue we were wrestling with. My tactic, in terms of trying to gauge what was right and what was wrong, was to try to listen to Elisa and figure out what might prove best for *her*. My thinking wasn't completely unselfish. The thing I was trying to avoid most was that the pregnancy—whether carried to term or terminated—would prove too much for our fledgling relationship to bear.

"What's most important to *me* is *us*," I told Elisa. "I want to do whatever gives *us* the best chance to stay together, because I've never felt so good about anyone I've been with before." Elisa visited her gynecologist to confirm the pregnancy test results. As the limited time within which we had to make a decision ticked away, I found myself concerned for Elisa whichever direction her emotions led her. At first she seemed to feel that having a child at the beginning of her life and career in the United States, not to mention at the very beginning of a relationship, would be a mistake. These thoughts often reversed themselves. I arrived home to find her reading books about pregnancy and child rearing. A good deal of the time Elisa would simply be feeling ill, or exhausted, or both. She spent many days and nights shifting between two activities: sleeping and crying.

Meanwhile, I was trekking through snowstorms to the theater. There I juggled calls with contractors, managed my own aching heart, and did my job—which was to make people laugh. The play I was performing in ended with me sandwiched between two women, one pretending to be pregnant, the other pretending to be dying. I'd make my way home to Elisa, where we'd discuss our thoughts and options deep into the night. One result of the crisis was that Elisa and I quickly grew closer and closer together. We spent every waking hour together talking about our lives, dreams, and desires. Instead of living separately and slowly getting to know each other, we spent every night sleeping in each other's arms.

It became clearer and clearer to me that I had found a woman who possessed the strength and like-mindedness I'd been hoping to locate my entire adult life. "In marriage, choose someone you're comfortable solving problems with" was an aphorism I'd been acquainted with. I had long ago concocted my own turbocharged version, which better fit my own history and worldview. The blessing to be carefully preserved, I'd concluded, is a partner with whom you'd not only be able to *endure* a crisis but whose companionship you could continue to enjoy *in spite of* the crisis. It became apparent that I might have found exactly that. Deciding which course of action would prove most likely to protect our union (or least likely to destroy it) would prove tougher to puzzle out.

Eventually I came to the conclusion that the way to best protect our chances for long-term happiness with each other would be to preserve our brand-new devotion to each other—and to each other alone. It would be horrific to participate in the destruction of a pregnancy I'd dreamed of and imagined as impossible. But I wanted to have *us*, even if it meant us alone, more than I wanted to have a child.

My primary concern, though, was still Elisa. I didn't want my leanings to influence her, should she feel more prepared for parenthood. Nor did I want her to give birth to a child out of concern for my "one in a million" prospects for fatherhood. The more I listened, the more it seemed that she wasn't ready for, much less fully committed to, parenthood at that moment, either. I shared my own reluctance to embark upon such a journey while still in the first stages of getting to know each other. For the moment we seemed to agree.

Then we started to talk to the doctors.

THE FIRST THING we learned from our calls to various experts (including the good people at Johns Hopkins Hospital who'd cared for me during my bone marrow transplant fifteen years earlier) was that the "one in a million" statistic I'd been quoted ten years before had been adjusted. Radically. Instead of the "one in a million" chance of achieving a conception I'd been quoted, about ten percent of the people who'd received treatment like me had since been known to regenerate fertility. From one in a million to one in ten. That's an adjustment of *a hundred thousand percent*. If I'd been an automobile I would have been recalled for safety reasons.

It was extraordinary news, and in almost every way it was wonderful. I felt as if I'd won a prize. I also wished I'd been warned that the prize might be in my possession, so I could have taken better care to keep from getting in trouble as a result of possessing it.

A NUMBER OF the women on the writing staff of *Sex and the City* used a gynecologist named Dr. Trask, who was also an obstetrician. I didn't want to broadcast the reason for our visit, so those we asked weren't able to cater their recommendations to our specific needs. We stated at the time we made an appointment with Dr. Trask's staff that we were seeking information about appropriate time frames for, and possible risks associated with, pregnancy terminations. We repeated the request in the doctor's pristine office, sitting side by side in front of his immaculately uncluttered desk. Unfortunately for Elisa and myself, the physician my colleagues had recommended was less than sympathetic toward our position.

"I'm not really crazy about abortion," was Dr. Trask's response. It turned out to be an understatement.

"Do you love each other?" he asked. "If you do, then what's the problem?"

I found his litmus test jarring. I was seeking the information we'd requested *because* I loved Elisa. But Dr. Trask had just begun.

"Pregnancy and childbirth is the highest calling you have as a woman," he announced to Elisa. "It's the purpose of your presence here on earth. I don't see what the problem is."

I knew how delicate Elisa's emotional state was. I felt extremely protective of her. I didn't want to stop her from weighing every aspect of the issue. I just didn't want her to be influenced by a stranger who was expressing views that had nothing to do with us as individuals. I wondered how to best extricate us from this consultation without intruding upon Elisa's prerogatives. Before I'd found an answer, the doctor instructed Elisa to follow him into an examination room. I had a dreadful suspicion of what was about to occur, but didn't know how to intervene without being guilty of interfering. I watched as she was led away.

I was invited to join her in an already darkened room where my fears were confirmed. Elisa was lying on her back, draped with sheets, while the doctor performed a sonogram. Elisa, tears running down her cheeks, was staring at the swooshing black and green glow of the monitor. The doctor was pointing out the barely distinguishable shape, curve, and outlines of the four-week-old embryo. (I'm dispensing with the LNMP, or "last normal menstrual period," dating method. Using LNMP, the embryo would commonly be referred to as having reached a gestational age of six weeks, even though conception would actually have occurred two weeks later than that. Don't ask me to explain how such a system developed.)

The monitor's volume was turned up high. The barely formed potential being inside Elisa's belly had no limbs, no discernible spine or brain, and no recognizable human form. But the rapid thwump, thwump, thwump of the heartbeat was immediately apparent and shockingly vital. I don't like to admit it, because those who find our inclinations to be amoral will seize on it, but what I saw on that screen was a very clear representation of life. Insentient, preconscious life. But I saw the brute force of life that was determined—indeed, whose sole purpose was—to stay alive. It was a primitive version of an instinct I was well acquainted with.

Elisa was shaken and upset as we left the doctor's office. I was shaken and enraged. I suspect there will be those (perhaps even a great number of those) who will feel the doctor did exactly what should be done under such circumstances. But he hadn't done what we'd asked. We came to him as private, paying customers. We explicitly requested medical information about the risks to future pregnancies should we decide to terminate the current one. Instead, he gave us a recitation of his own views about the purpose of a woman's existence. He performed a medically unnecessary procedure, giving us a wildly magnified glimpse of something it should have been our choice to view or not. Personally, I'd rather not have heard the robust heartbeat of what I regard as a form of life, yes—just as everything from a single skin cell in a petri dish to a tree fungus to an elephant is a form of life. But I see it only as the most meager precursor to the potential for a human being. Or maybe I'd rather not have seen it because I'm aware of how precious and precarious the underlying force behind it is.

We left the office with an indelible image burned into our brains. We also had the name and number of another doctor whose views— and methods and manner—were drastically different from those of the one we'd just left. That turned out to be something both good and utterly bizarre.

DR. PLATT WAS an elfin, elderly gentleman whose office was as worn and unkempt as Dr. Trask's had been spare and immaculate. The room had a ramshackle feel similar to the one given off by the doctor himself. His disorganized desk had cartoonish ceramic figures of storks, and of bundled babies on scales. The office walls were jammed with photographs of mothers and children that seemed to travel up to the present from decades past. Dr. Platt had an obvious devotion to delivering and nurturing healthy children. He also offered immediate understanding of those who might not feel prepared, or equipped, to choose that path.

"You've got plenty of time," the doctor said after hearing Elisa's age. "The last thing you want to do is to have a child when you're not ready. It's a serious undertaking. When you're ready I'm sure you'll make fantastic parents."

Dr. Platt made a sweeping gesture toward the photos on the walls surrounding us. "As you can see, we've helped a number of people already. When you're ready, we'll be happy to help you join them. When you're ready."

The doctor gave us a demonstration of the termination procedure, illustrating his description on a plastic model of the female reproductive organs. His description was as bereft of any connection to its connotations as the prior doctor's had been overburdened by them. There was something about the man's pride in his expertise in the procedure that was unnerving. We were glad to have the right to it, but we still viewed it as solemn and sad.

For all his warmth and comfort, Dr. Platt was an odd little man. The office's whimsical decor and playful demeanor carried over into the tiny, aged surgical suite, which seemed more than strange. Staring down from the ceiling at the gurney upon which his patients would lie was a two-by-three-foot poster, mounted behind Plexiglas, of a photograph of Clint Eastwood from *Two Mules for Sister Sara*. The actor was wrapped in a poncho, and topped by a cowboy hat. His eyes squinted and his teeth clenched a cigarette. Clint's eyes were positioned to stare directly into those of whoever lay beneath.

"It's for my patients," the doctor quipped. "I find it helps them to relax."

I swear, I think I saw him wink when he said it.

Even more troubling was his sympathetic and extremely tall Nordic nurse. In a moment of privacy, she tried to comfort Elisa by confiding that she'd had five abortions herself. I'd wanted to find a place where our needs would be met in a respectful, professional manner. I didn't want a joint where abortion was made fun of, or where it had become a hobby.

AFTER A BRIEF period of vacillation and introspection, Elisa and I made our decision to terminate the pregnancy. We wanted the procedure performed as early in the pregnancy as possible, well within the first trimester, and found it impossible to gain appointments with additional physicians within that time. Despite some reservations, we scheduled the procedure with cheery Dr. Platt, who was able to accommodate our haste.

Elisa lay on her back on the table. The strange little man perched on a stool between her legs. The woman who'd had five abortions of her own held one of Elisa's hands. I sat by Elisa's other side, holding her other hand. Clint Eastwood, squinting as if at the sun, grimaced down on us all.

I was still torn about the decision. It was hard for me to believe, as the procedure started, that I had let things come to this.

How could I have let this happen? I thought.

But I hadn't "let it happen." I'd chosen it.

IN A CASE of questionable morality of a much lesser sort, Moti refused to refund the money that had been paid to him prior to his demolition of my apartment's floors. When nothing else worked, I went to small-claims court for the city of New York and filed a lawsuit against him. Weeks later, after Elisa's termination procedure, I found myself waiting in a hearing room to present my case to one of the volunteer lawyers who act as judges in such cases. Elisa was with me, since she had been a witness to our dealings and to the floor's condition.

Moti made a dramatic entrance. His wife, who was now seven and a half months pregnant, accompanied him. She had witnessed none of our dealings, and had never entered the apartment in question. Moti held her arm as he escorted her into the room. He helped ease her into her seat. Elisa and I glanced at each other, commenting silently on the irony of our comparative situations, as well as Moti's blatant attempt to garner sympathy by parading out his pregnant wife. I presented my case to the man who acted as our judge, displaying photographs of the ruined floor and the canceled checks for the money I'd paid.

When it was Moti's turn to offer evidence, he told a story that was unrecognizable to me. In front of me and Elisa, in front of the man acting as the judge, in front of whoever or whatever powers might look down upon such proceedings, and in front of his very pregnant wife, he distorted facts, invented events and conversations, and made up excuses. He insisted that, as the contractor I'd hired, it was his right to repair any damage he'd caused. He stated not only that he didn't owe me any money back but that I still owed him for the balance of the job. Eventually the arbitrator seemed to lose patience.

"Mr. Nassirim," the arbitrator interrupted. "What about these lines in the floor? Do you see these photographs? How did these deep lines get carved into that floor?"

"Those lines were there before I started," Moti said.

MY NOTICE OF victory in the lawsuit arrived in the mail the next day. Winners of lawsuits in New York small-claims court are required to attempt to collect their judgments on their own. I didn't have a lot of faith that Moti was suddenly going to pay, but my prediction proved wrong. In a further illustration that morality is defined differently by different people, Moti made plans to meet me at my bank.

"Yes, Evan," he said. "The court has decided, so I'm going to pay."

When we met, after he'd handed over an envelope filled with cash,

Moti wanted to shake my hand. "I'm sorry it worked out this way," he said.

Sorry for what? I thought. Was he sorry that he'd ruined my floor? Sorry he'd cost me thousands of dollars, and days and weeks of time while I was wrestling with much more serious issues? Was he sorry while he lied in front of Elisa, the judge, and his pregnant wife? Or was he sorry only because, as the official loser, he was now expected to be? I didn't ask, and I'll never know. Even with an explanation, I don't believe I'd understand.

I arrived home from the bank to the freshly painted Eighty-ninth Street apartment. The floors had already been repaired and refinished, and all my furniture had arrived from Los Angeles. Elisa and I had been living there together for months already. The result of all the turmoil and sorrow was that we became solidified as a couple. A team. We were no longer individuals investigating each other, but people who'd decided to fuse themselves into something larger than either one of us could have been on our own. I suppose that's something like what parenthood might have been like. But it was accomplished by our avoidance of that.

There are moments when I'll wonder what kind of child might have been living with us, had we made another choice. I've wondered whether there's a soul that was formed upon conception that was never allowed to live and breathe. There are also times when I remind myself that there is no certainty that such an early-stage pregnancy would ever have "become" anything. Somewhere between 50 and 75 percent of fertilized human eggs spontaneously abort without anyone knowing a pregnancy ever existed. A full 15 percent of even confirmed pregnancies end in miscarriage. I've got a friend whose thirty-five-year-old wife recently gave birth to twins. She very nearly died from uncontrollable hemorrhaging shortly after giving birth. Surgeons were forced to remove her uterus and cervix after five hours of surgery failed to stop the bleeding. She'd already lost three-fifths of her body's blood and suffered some form of mild heart attack during the crisis. The risks of even the most intended pregnancies are real. There are no guarantees of anything, for anyone. Elisa and I chose to make the preservation of our new union our first priority. I believe that choice has allowed it to flourish. When, or if, we do have children, we will have a solid foundation between the two of us, established as a result of years of stability. We'll have a deeper knowledge of each other than we ever could have had as the near-strangers we were. We'll be able to set consistent examples for whoever we might come to raise, with trust, and faith, and confidence—in ourselves, and in each other.

That's not to completely dismiss what we did. I feel bad about it. Allowing the situation to happen was a mistake, and one from which we'll never completely recover. But when viewed on the universal scale of sin, I believe ours was a small one, and one for which I hope to be forgiven. If not by higher powers, then at least by other people. If not forgiven by every one of them, at least forgiven by myself.

You Don't Know Where You Are,

Until You're Somewhere Else

BEREFT. That word could pretty much serve as the caption for any snapshot taken of me in my thirties. A decade entered as a traumatized refugee, who'd already experienced old age and dying, though somehow managed to escape death itself. I lived like a man on the run, and in nearly every respect—romantically, financially, psychically—I exited the decade on a lower plane than that on which I'd entered. But as the alcoholic in recovery will tell you, the bottom is the blessing. Because the only place to go from there is up.

Things are different now. Regret has been replaced by contentment. It used to be that the urge to go back and redo, or correct, was stronger than the urge to be wherever I was. It's not that I don't ever have the desire to revisit anything anymore. Only that the pleasure I get from being exactly where I am is now stronger than the desire for whatever was, or whatever might have been. That, to me, is contentment. And that, for me, is new.

. . .

WHICH MAKES ME wonder whether any of my perceptions from earlier eras were accurate. I don't mean to take anything back, or to suggest it's not the way things were at the time. Only that they're no longer so. Reality, it seems, alters as we do.

I'm not one of those "create your own reality" people. We don't change the truth of what once was. Time does. Since we're stapled to our particular strand of that entity it's all but impossible to comprehend time's structure. I've only been able to imagine brief glimpses beyond my particular place in line. There probably have been those in history, and some living today, more gifted at sensing the scope of what's beyond their immediate perceptual grasps. Buddhist masters, perhaps. Bob Dylan, maybe—though, Lord knows, he won't be sharing any of his secrets anytime soon. But to know where you are, while you're there, is one of the universe's purest blessings. It's also (for me) one of its most rare.

The new perspective I've gained hasn't just added meaning to events, it's *altered* their meaning. It's clear to me now that I shouldn't have pressured myself to make *any* of the relationships I've obsessed over here work beyond the time they did. In most cases I shouldn't have mourned their passing. They were learning experiences. Some were necessary as stepping-stones toward the better days that have come. Some were nonessential. None were relationships that stood a chance of enduring.

My progress toward maturity might have been lethargic, but it's inaccurate to state (as I already have) that anything was "my fault." I might have owed my ex-fiancée Patricia certain apologies. But we failed together. The last time I saw her was years after our split, and over a very friendly lunch she agreed. She told me of the techniques she'd since embraced to help her learn to communicate more openly than she'd previously been able. She even offered some apologies of her own.

None of my relationships were done in by my imperfect behavior alone, regardless of what I felt at the time. They failed because we weren't compatible as couples. Each of the women was probably just as crazy as I've made her out to be. But none of them was any crazier than me.

I have a hard time these days connecting to many of the feelings I had in the past. When I think back on the years with Patricia, I feel none of the pain, regret, or sadness that once consumed me. I don't find any of the depressing stories upsetting, or any of the "most proud moments" and "best man I ever was"-es contained in this collection still accurate. I certainly no longer have videotaped records of our time together. I threw those out long ago. Not in a purging ceremony or as an attempt to expunge their power. They no longer had any. They'd become relics whose potency had diminished to the point of being irretrievable. Imagine that. Being unable to conjure something I once couldn't escape. Without medication. Which I no longer view as "the best thing that ever happened to me." Elisa is.

In one of the more perfect metaphorical moments of my life, the red KitchenAid mixer I'd bought for Patricia made a clunking sound and expired the first time my Italian wife and I used it together to make pasta. I think it knew its time had passed. Would that I'd had such a keen sense of timing in terms of my own relationships when I was younger.

I'VE GOT THE same reversal of feelings when I think back on Abbey Leigh. If I could go back and correct anything there, it would be that I never would have come back from Australia when I did. I wouldn't have remained faithful to a dysfunctional relationship back home for two torturous months, only to spend an additional year in emotional exile on my return. I would have lived with the woman most available to me at the time, and most crucial to my own development. We wouldn't have enjoyed a different destiny, but we could have indulged our hunger for what we had to offer each other in less restricted fashion. The mistake wasn't in pursuing the intensity of our desire. It was in walking away in order to conform to a preconceived notion of responsible behavior. What I once thought was the truth of the experience has been revealed to be a distortion.

I look back in amazement at how much I tortured myself, over even casual dates. Now I just think how much more fun I could have had with all those crazy encounters if I'd known my wife was destined to appear. I wouldn't have felt bad when any particular evening was a disaster, or even when a full-fledged relationship fell apart. I would have just thought, Hey, on to the next. Because I would have known. I would have trusted that, eventually, the one I want will come along.

Faith. A pretty handy item.

Frivolous engagement rings, fury at missionary physicians, less-than-perfect sperm banks. Badly timed kisses, bad behavior in relationships, badly run races. It's not that I can't remember how I felt. It's just that the feelings are no longer alive. They're memories. I make the distinction here because the distinction, for me, wasn't always clear.

The red car I wrote of as being the only one I'd ever owned has since become merely my "first." My ten-year-old nephew who exhibited such insight when things with Patricia fell apart is now seventeen. I feel none of the regrets I once so freely expressed, and crave none of the forgiveness I once felt was needed. In retrospect, I don't believe any crimes were even committed. Even the celebrity status that suddenly appeared will, itself, eventually expire. *Everything* has changed, or else will soon enough. In what's probably the most profound adjustment to my existence, loneliness—which had seeped into my bones and informed every choice in every story I've told—has vanished from my life. It's as difficult for me to remember its ache now as it was to escape it just a few years ago. Nothing now feels the way it once did. That sentence contains the happiest facts of my life.

I DO WONDER whether time is the only ingredient that alters perception, and whether its passage alters every one. Eight months after the termination of a pregnancy, Elisa Atti and I were married, in a nonreligious two-language ceremony at our favorite restaurant in New York. Her bewildered Italian parents sat next to my East Coast American Jewish parents in a circular red-leather booth. The day before, in the same room, they'd watched as their daughter was photographed with her television star fiancé for *O: The Oprah Magazine*.

The wedding meant we'd succeeded in preserving our union. Whether we'd have remained together, or as happy, having made other choices, we'll never know. I still feel regret over what we decided was necessary then. That regret will grow or fade depending on what the future holds. There's no way to know from here. Because you don't know where you are, you never know where you are, until you're somewhere else.

THE YEARS SINCE our wedding have been like a fairy tale filled with comedic collisions between cultures. We've moved from New York, where wealth is relatively hidden from view and rich and poor swirl together in a roiling mix, to Santa Monica, California, where wealth is flaunted by those who have it and the classes are as segregated as anywhere I've ever been. We're not always happy with every detail of our lives, but we are happy with each other. I am happy, finally, to be exactly where I am.

I know there's no guarantee my newfound happiness will be permanent. I'm better equipped to maintain healthy perspectives, but I'm smart enough to know that the universe could lay me down with the most casual of blows. "Faith," as traditionally defined, still lies beyond my grasp. I wonder if that's contradictory when I expose the most contradictory fact: I pray, nearly every day. To whom, I'm not sure. I stand by my statement of "I Don't Know." But I do send requests. I give thanks. Just in case. Like thank-you cards. I've yet to have an important plea denied.

I WONDER, now that my relationship to trust has changed, if I could ever go through an ordeal as serious as my illness and simply trust that everything will be all right. The experiences that could be proof that I should feel safe and protected are the same experiences that prove what danger lies all around. Those same experiences also indicate how much can be overcome. What am I to conclude?

Simplistic conclusions, like absolute faith and trust, are still beyond my capabilities. But I have learned that whatever threats might still be lurking are only trails to be traveled until a new path appears. There is no arrival point. Only a journey, then a passage from which no one's ever sent back any reports. My philosophy these days is summed up best by what my friend Jackie once told me. She was trying to ease my pain over one of my many overblown heartbreaks.

"It's only temporary, Ev," Jackie said.

"Yeah, so is everything," I responded.

"Well, that's the good news and the bad news, then, isn't it?"

And so it is.

On Death and Dying

MY WIFE, ELISA, and I were strolling in Santa Monica's Palisades Park recently, looking out over the Pacific Ocean. The park is a narrow strip of green grass and shade, with towering palm trees, that stretches for two miles or so along Ocean Avenue. The Pacific Coast Highway buzzes next to the ocean a couple of hundred feet below the cliffs that line the park's western edge. The park is filled with well-to-do, intimidatingly (or inspirationally, depending on your perspective) fit people walking dogs, performing tai chi, practicing yoga, or lying together on blankets having some form of fully clothed public sex. The views are spectacular, whether of the multimillion-dollar apartments that line the avenue, the glittering ocean, the Santa Monica Mountains above Malibu, or—on the days when the air is clear enough—Catalina Island smoldering in the mist off the coast of Long Beach. It's a nice place to take a walk, and one of the more significant reasons we relocated from New York City.

On this particular evening, while taking in the sights we depend on to relax and inspire us, we were talking about death. My wife and I talk about death a lot. We also talk about illness, disaster, war, and calamities of widely assorted natures. But they all really add up to the same thing. It's death we're always talking about, or referring to, however obliquely. Either that, or the only thing worse: unrelenting suffering.

These conversations aren't confined to our walks in the park. The ease and luxury of a fabulous dinner with my wife is often followed by a chat about . . . what? The sadness of sex for those who are HIV positive, the aftermath of earthquakes, the heartbreak to come for whichever of us dies last. Or first. What it will feel like as we slip away, realizing we're doomed and are forced to say good-bye. Or we'll discuss a story about someone else who's fallen into whatever horrifying state frightens us the most, and we'll say: "Oh, no. That's the worst. That's really one of the worst things that can happen to you." Yes, it's a serene picnic as Elisa and I lounge around the house.

That's just our conversation. As much as I've succeeded in distancing myself from my past, my private fantasy life is worse. Every day I think I'm having a heart attack. Every day. Every time I cross a street I imagine an approaching car smashing into me, tearing me apart. Every time. Cancer. Every day. Aortic aneurysm. A steel beam from above, if I'm walking under one. Melanoma. Neuroblastoma. I imagine what it'll feel like when my heart explodes. My brain hemorrhages. Blood spews from my mouth. The doctor tells me my life is over. Again. Which in my case means for the third or fourth time.

I fantasize about my own death constantly. I'm no longer referring to momentary imaginings of strokes, heart attacks, car crashes, stabbings, shootings, impalings, or eviscerations. I'm talking about extended daydreams of a concrete diagnosis, followed by a period of informing a selection of close friends. Then come fruitless interventions, ultimately resulting in deterioration, disfigurement, and a varied assortment of final moments. Usually, I'll concentrate on the reaction of one friend at a time. Occasionally it'll be my wife. Sometimes my mood in these reveries is stoically resigned, other times my anger burns hot and white. Always, though, the emotion outside the dream is unadulterated terror.

When I'm conversing with an acquaintance on the street and I feel a wisp of a breeze on my upper lip, I imagine blood is leaking from my nose. Really, I do. My ears. My eyes. An audition. Job interview. I feel my intestines rupture, my appendix burst. When I go to the gym to exercise, when I'm riding the stationary bike, should a trickle of sweat tickle my thigh, I think shit is leaking out of my ass. I have to go into the bathroom, lock the door, and check to make sure. It's always a false alarm. Still, ten minutes later, I go back to check again.

People wonder why I seem distracted, or why I don't remember their names after we've met. I want to tell them, "Because I was having a heart attack while we spoke." Would that excuse my lack of concentration? "An aneurysm, a stroke, a bowel movement. You didn't know it was happening, but that's what was going on with me. In the privacy of my mind. I'm terribly sorry. Could you tell me your story again?"

It wouldn't make any difference. Not if there was a thunderstorm I could imagine electrocuting me, an airplane passing that might land on me, or anyone, anywhere, I cared about that I could conceive of being murdered in some horrible fashion. It's not that I don't want to listen. It's just that, sometimes, it's hard. Like, every day. Every single instant of every single day.

Then there's the fact that I hardly ever sleep.

EVEN MORE DEBILITATING than those residual effects of my distant traumas are the more "legitimate" health scares. In the eighteen years since my bone marrow transplant, at least once or twice a year, one or several physicians become concerned about some possibly life-threatening development or complication from past medical treatments. Bladder cancer, lymphoma (Hodgkin's and non-Hodgkin's both, thank you very much), colon cancer, testicular cancer, brain matter crystallization. When I got through with specifically male and/or gender neutral diseases, I started having scares resembling traditionally female disorders. Yes, I have submitted to a breast needle biopsy, out of concern on the parts of several physicians over an ovoid lump near my left nipple. It turned out to consist of—brace yourselves—fat.

Panic is what I experience during these episodes. That's *after* the four years of living that way every day, with good reason and concrete justification. Compared to those days, the concerns over the last decade and a half have been quaint. But I'm *tired,* man.

The requirements for soothing my distress have become increasingly stringent. It used to require only a visit to a doctor or a blood test to lay my fears to rest. Now it's reached a point where only a biopsy of suspect tissues or a detailed computer tomography scan will reassure me. The time might not be far off when it'll take an autopsy to calm me down.

Every so often I apologize to my wife for my expectation that I'm going to die young and leave her alone. Actually, I don't apologize for the expectation. I apologize to her, in advance, for what I see as the *inevitability* that I'll come down with an incurable illness, or die suddenly, leaving her alone, or with whatever children we might have. I vacillate between grieving over how costly these apprehensions have been in terms of time, dollars, and psychic energy and marveling at how much I've been able to accomplish in spite of them.

If I'm this crazy, I sometimes wonder, how crazy are real crazy people? I consider my own level of anxiety to be substantial (and wouldn't you?), yet thoughts of suicide never cross my mind. My anxieties are all centered on the overwhelming desire to hold *on to* life. But is there a point where anxiety over, and fear of, death makes some people choose to hasten it? Do some people kill themselves, not because they don't want to live, but because they can no longer take the suspense of not knowing when or how they're going to die?

If so, there's good news at last. I haven't gotten there. Not yet. What

I want is *more.* More life. Just like when I was clawing and clutching to preserve my existence. Only now, because my life is so much better, I want more even more than I used to.

It's nice to have found someone in Elisa who understands and can tolerate my obsessions. My insanity's got hers beat by about a hundred thousand kilometers, but she's got enough of the bug to empathize. She's even got a sense of humor about it. After reading a book that suggests people can sense, and hasten, the approach of their own deaths, I told Elisa, "Reading this makes me afraid I'm going to die soon."

"No, no, no," Elisa said reassuringly. "If your thoughts could kill you, you'd be dead a long time already."

I IMAGINE I'D feel differently now about losing a battle to stay alive than I would have in my midtwenties. My relationship to suffering hasn't changed in the years since my illness, but my relationship to the notion of death has. It wasn't altered by my close encounters with it. It's been altered by my wife.

When I was sick, I spent a lot of time imagining what my response might be were I to learn that my battle was lost, and that my life was coming to an end. I wondered whether I'd be able to release the anger I'd carried (and that had carried me) through. Would I be able to come to some degree of acceptance? I always concluded that the question was either irrelevant or poorly phrased. It wasn't so much that I wouldn't be *able* to attain such an unburdened state, but that I wouldn't *want* to. If I was going to go at twenty-four, twenty-five, or twenty-six years old, I thought, I'm going to go out kicking and screaming. I'm going to die in a full-blown temper tantrum. I'll never accept, or cooperate with, the travesty being committed upon me. Talk about a sense of entitlement.

Now, at forty-five, my inclinations are different. Not because I'd be any less terrified. Because I feel more fulfilled.

First, there would be the obvious sense that, having barely escaped what was represented as an almost certain death well before reaching thirty, I've been lucky just to get the extra fifteen or twenty years that have allowed me to reach forty-five. Middle age isn't old age, and it's still most often viewed as tragic when someone under fifty dies. But it sure beats the hell out of dying at twenty-five.

There's also a more complete sense of accomplishment. On a deep and intensely personal level, having had my opinions in regard to illness and health care seriously considered has been gratifying. On a shallower level, I have been fortunate enough to take part in one or more professional projects that have allowed me to experience some degree of recognition and acclaim. I can imagine letting go being easier having at least had a taste of each.

Ultimately, though, I've come to the conclusion that it doesn't matter one bit when we die. We're all going to. It's what we're *supposed* to do. If you've got a hot date scheduled, or maybe reservations at a restaurant that's really hard to get into, you'll probably want to put it off for a week or two. But beyond that, is tomorrow so much better than today? In the full sweep of history, is next year better than the current one? (Parents of young children are given full license to disagree.)

But none of those thoughts address what's really changed in my life and in my spirit. The critical factor is that I've found a mate. I have formed, and been fused into, a fulfilling partnership. The sense of completion that's given me has altered my emotional makeup and my relationship to my own mortality. It's given me a sense of a life well lived, and the feeling I'd be able to depart with less rancor than I ever would have before.

I'M MORE WILLING to face the end of my life having finally found pleasure in it. There's a hint of incongruity there, to say the least. And the thought prompts another fear. If I don't feel that death would be so terrible anymore, I worry I'm doing something nearly as dangerous as inviting it in. Analyze that, and you can see why someone like me might be invested in not enjoying himself very much. As long as I'm miserable about leaving a life in which I haven't yet found fulfillment, I'll fight hard enough to get to keep living the life that's not giving me what I want. On the other hand, if I get too happy and content, and don't fear death anymore due to a sense of fulfillment, I might be more likely to let it reach out and grab me. So I'd better stay miserable. That's the mixed-up form of common sense I've lived with and have had to learn to talk myself out of on a regular basis.

No longer feeling deprived, I can, at long last, experience gratitude. I am grateful. I am grateful for the time Elisa and I have spent together. I'm grateful simply for the miraculous experience of having found each other. I'm grateful for the years I've had, and for the shifts in perspective they've allowed that, in turn, have allowed me to see so many past events in less painful, regretful ways. I am deeply grateful, sincerely grateful, and purely grateful. As a result, I find I could now, as they say in some sentimental movies, die a happy man.

I sometimes wonder whether children would adjust the equation again. What if Elisa and I now had a two-month-old? A two-year-old? Or a child who was twelve? Would my feelings be different?

Of course the answer is yes. Because everything changes everything. Even as I write these words, I know they'll be at least somewhat inaccurate upon publication. If you want to know exactly how I feel about anything right now, give me a call. Better yet, show up at a bookstore appearance, and bring along twelve or thirteen of your closest friends.

A FACT THAT's lost within my private debate is that *I'm not actually dying right now*. At least not any more rapidly than anyone else. Unless someone has some test results I'm not aware of. I say to Elisa on our Palisades Park "death walks" all the time, "Not everyone spends so much time thinking about these things." I'm pretty sure most of the people around us overlooking the Pacific Ocean are floating more calmly through their days. It's true, at least half of them have had cosmetic surgery, and they're exercising with the demonic energy of those who want to stay twenty-one forever. They must sense something chasing them. But I think they're channeling their fears in more constructive ways. Or maybe they just stayed on their antidepressants longer.

I have met some people who went through trials like I did back in my midtwenties, but few of them admit to still being consumed by them. I've even heard some say, "I don't really think about those things anymore. That was then, this is now."

I used to be suspicious, finding those explanations less than credible. Then I met my wife, a woman who's got no reason to feel the specter of death and disaster as vividly as I do. The fact that she does, without any apparent provocation, indicates to me that the people who should, but don't, might be telling the truth. Damn them all to hell.

ONE OF THE better antidotes I found along the way, before the actual gratitude took root, was a kind of enforced gratitude. "Thinking of those less fortunate than oneself," I believe the technique is called. I'd tell myself, I could have had an illness that really was incurable, not just called incurable. I could have come down with amyotrophic lateral sclerosis—Lou Gehrig's disease. There's no ten percent recovery rate there to confuse the issue. There's only Stephen Hawking. And he can't be said to have recovered, only to have halted the progress of the illness by fusing himself with a computer to become the first superintelligent humanoid machine.

I could have been hit by a truck. There wouldn't have been any questions about luck, or cures, or God then. I would have been obliterated, a few humans would have grieved, and the earth would have continued to spin without me. I'm not a quadriplegic. I'm not home-less. Not an imprisoned Chinese intellectual. Those thoughts have all worked pretty well, at one time or another.

But now I'm able to turn to a new form of gratitude that's not forced. I'm able to look up above my desk to see the photograph of my wife leaping into my arms the moment we'd finished uttering our "I do's." Or the photo next to it, in which I'm casting a glance toward the wedding photographer, looking as pleased as if I'd just won an Acad-emy Award. I can open up files of photographs on my computer to see Elisa and myself smiling and enjoying ourselves in Italy, in Hawaii, at the Grand Canyon, in Big Sur. I can know that, even if I were inca-pable of experiencing joy other than through revenge, I'm getting what I've always heard was the best kind: I'm living well.

THAT WAS A time of war. I don't see what else you could call it. But now it's a different era. When Elisa and I wrote our wedding vows we each included a pledge she repeated to me recently. I was feeling anxious and frightened for no reason, acting clingy and babyish, and I apolo-gized. I thanked her for being so patient with me.

"I am your ally," she said. "Don't you remember? It's what we promised in our vows. I am your ally."

Of course, with her accent she pronounced it uh-*lie.* "I am your uh-*lie.*" So it took me a few seconds to understand. But when I did, I knew for sure not only how far I'd traveled but where it is that I've arrived. Yes, I fought a war. It was long ago, but its residue remains. But when I think of Elisa. When I smile the same smile now that I smiled the day I met her. When the smile pops involuntarily over my face, itself a rec-ognizable friend, every time she crosses my mind. Every single time. Or when I roll toward her in bed—our nest, we like to call it, to remind ourselves of the animals we are—and I simply place the knuckles of one hand against her warm skin, I feel a comfort as strong as any threat I've ever faced, and I know what it is I've found. Not only happiness. Not only joy. Not only gratitude, though it includes them all. I've found what I was seeking even before I endured its opposite. I've found peace.

I've found peace. And it feels good.

WHEN BLEAK THOUGHTS come anyway, when I find I can't quite dispatch them and the best I can hope for is to counterpunch effectively, I've now got thoughts to turn to that offer as much comfort and protection as the fear the dark ones instill.

"I am your uh-*lie*," I hear Elisa telling me. "I am your uh-*lie*."

And, I swear—if only for ten or fifteen minutes—it makes me feel safe all over again.

The End Is the Beginning

(of the Beginning of the End)

Ever since the pregnancy Elisa and I confronted early in our relationship we'd had concerns about whether we'd be able to accomplish anything like it on purpose. Just this past year we decided to investigate how difficult a path toward parenthood might prove to be, so I made an appointment to have my sperm tested. We wanted to confirm our suspicion that I was one of the lucky ten percent whose sperm production had regenerated in the years since my medical treatments.

I drove myself to a strip mall in the San Fernando Valley where, after passing from my air-conditioned car through the brutal desert heat, I entered a nondescript medical office building. In suite number 302 a gruff Russian woman solicited information from me. The woman then handed me a key and a tiny, lidded plastic container. She directed me down the hall, where I let myself into a storage-closet-sized room.

A reclining chair dominated the space. Facing the chair, uncomfortably close, was a television/VCR console with a videocassette dangling perilously from its lips. I looked down at the chair, the only place in the room to sit. The impressions of countless buttocks had worn dual tread marks into its upholstered surface. I sat down and pushed the videocassette into the machine's mouth. Some of the most dispiriting pornography I've ever seen assaulted my senses.

I'm no prude. I have a healthy appreciation for certain stripes of pornography. I believe there are a limited number of films that depict actual pleasure exchanged between healthy individuals. The movie at this fertility clinic did not fall into this category.

What I saw were obese, seemingly drug-addicted people whose disinterest shrieked off the screen. They were plodding through gyrations in zombie-like states. You'd think a fertility clinic in the pornography capital of the world would have something better than the dregs of the genre. I snapped the television off.

The first masturbatorium (as they're known in the andrology industry) I'd entered twenty years earlier had been furnished with a utilitarian metal folding chair. I'd found that choice inconsiderate. Faced with the faded recliner, I had to admit to its equal impracticality. Remember, the object of the game is to get a few milliliters of viscous fluid, coaxed out of one's body via strenuous manipulation, into an impossibly small container. Lying on one's back, or even reclining slightly, is not the most gravitationally efficacious position for delivery unto the cup. Hunching forward at the furnishing's edge doesn't make it much easier. Neither does standing up. Truth be told, there's no elegant way of going about it. It's a damned difficult job.

I did succeed. I drove home with instructions to phone the doctor's office later that afternoon. I was pleasantly surprised to get a call from the doctor before the appointed time. I was less pleasantly startled to learn the results. My sperm count was unchanged from eighteen years earlier. It was as dismal as it had been immediately after my bone marrow transplant, when I'd been quoted the "one in a million" statistic. The total count was barely one-tenth of the amount considered the lowest end of the normal range, with an especially poor percentage of normally formed specimens. The doctor wasn't opposed to Elisa and my going ahead and trying to conceive without interventions, but he was less than optimistic about our chances.

"I wouldn't give it any more than a couple of cycles," he said.

THE SUPPOSITION I'D clung to to lessen my grief over our choice to abort a pregnancy three years earlier was snatched away. The assumption I'd made in regard to the rarity of that pregnancy was revealed as what it was: rationalization. No one had given me any evidence that my fertility had recovered since my medical treatments. I'd only been given the information that such recoveries had occurred. Yet, I'd seized on it as proof of my own restoration. I spent the rest of the afternoon grieving over the loss of something I'd believed was gained only three years earlier, but that had never actually been mine. Perhaps for the first time I mourned the loss of a child that had never been allowed to live.

Elisa came home from work excited and expecting good news. "Did you get the results?" she asked.

"I'm afraid they weren't good."

"What do you mean?"

"The count was low."

"How low?"

"About as low as you can get without being gone."

We acknowledged the probability of having to consult fertility specialists when we were ready to conceive. We speculated again on the viability of the frozen semen that was now twenty years old. We offered each other comfort and pledges of love and commitment. We handled things in all the best ways. But none of that changed the fact that we were very shaken, and extremely sad.

The next day Elisa reached for me in the midst of a sun-dappled afternoon nap. We'd had an indulgent homemade lunch, during which I'd uncharacteristically helped myself to two or three doses of wine during daylight hours. In spite of the buzz, and the sun, and the beautiful companion, I felt reluctant to make love. Making love reminded me of my sadness from the day before, and my sadness was doubled over the fact that one of our most carefree activities had become infected with grief. I overrode my resistance, and Elisa and I had sex.

I found it difficult to stay present. My mind fluctuated between sorrowful thoughts and flash-fantasies of fertilizing demonic beings. It wasn't one of the most beautiful erotic experiences of my life. I found myself hoping—in spite of my knowledge that I was incapable of impregnating anyone—that no conception would result from such a session.

I didn't share those thoughts with Elisa. I played along over the next few days as she began making jokes about what we both knew were impossible symptoms, all experienced within premature time frames. Elisa started to drop comments about tender breasts and abdominal rumblings within forty-eight hours of making love. Only eleven days after that, as we frolicked again in Santa Monica's Palisades Park, Elisa startled me with an announcement.

"I bought a pregnancy test today."

I'd begun to wonder at the persistence of the symptoms she'd been describing for two weeks. I was concerned as to whether Elisa might be in some kind of denial of the facts. I drove us home, trying to figure out how to handle her disappointment when it arrived.

Elisa went into the bathroom alone, as she'd done three years before. She called me to join her only seconds later in a voice that was reminiscent of the one I'd heard on Forty-ninth Street in New York. With hands that were again trembling, she passed me the slender plastic stick, with one bright pink preprinted band, and another paler one staring insistently back at us. We held the test capsule up to the light, and compared it over and over to the pictures printed on its instruction page. We tried as best we could to find disparities between the illustration for "positive" and the test we were holding in our hands.

"Why is the second line so much paler than the first?" we asked each other.

"What does it matter? The second line is paler in the diagram, too."

"But this is impossible," we said. And we giggled. We giggled because we didn't know what else to do, or how to proceed with anything in the face of what seemed to be, but couldn't be, happening.

We did the only thing we could think of, which was to tear open a second test and do it over again. The second test came back as positive as the first, just as the first had been as positive as the one three years earlier. Elisa was pregnant. We'd had sex without using birth control twice in our entire relationship, and—in spite of a sperm count that's supposed to make such a thing all but impossible—each time resulted in a conception. That's an astounding occurrence. It's one in a million, twice in a row.

This time, after three years of marriage, we're ecstatic. We've giggled, laughed and cried, hugged, and stopped repeatedly to gasp in wonder. We haven't been able to stop shaking our heads. We haven't known what to say. We don't understand how such a thing could have happened. Twice. We've moved in haste to a larger home where we've prepared a nursery. We've had perfect sonograms, a clear amniocentesis, and on January 17, 2007, Sofia Clementina Handler was born.

Reproduction is a magical, mystical process, even under the least surprising of circumstances. Miraculous, some would say. If every conception, and every birth, is a miracle, what does that make our baby?

WE GOT TO the hospital four hours into Elisa's labor. There I witnessed something I'd never experienced. I saw medical care administered with all the gallantry, haste, and heroism we're led to expect from television shows like *ER.* Everything I'd hoped for, but never seen, during my extended health crisis twenty years earlier was on display. At UCLA Medical Center, any woman who presents at the emergency room more than twenty weeks pregnant is immediately sent up to the labor and delivery floor. No waiting. Heart attack patients wait. Stabbing victims wait. Gunshot wounds wait. Pregnant women are given a wheelchair and an escort, and are taken directly to the elevator. (This is the plus side of a more troubling fact: that same woman, a week after delivery, would be treated with less urgency for more serious conditions. Once that baby's born, neither she nor her mother will get such swift treatment again. We learned this the hard way with postpartum problems ten days later.)

Before a catheter could be inserted into Elisa's spinal column, through which her epidural pain relief would flow, the physicians needed to get her "informed consent" for the procedure. A young resident read his required text faster than the most distracted flight attendant has ever sped through the safety features of an aircraft.

"Doyouunderstandthateverymedicalprocedurecarriestheriskof complications?"

But here the speed wasn't due to indifference. It was due to a genuine desire to rapidly provide Elisa with the relief she'd requested. The resident paused while Elisa endured a contraction, then read the next batch of text as if he were speaking in tongues. Within ten minutes she was relaxed and pain-free.

I WAS PRESENT for my daughter's birth. This was a surprise, as I'm squeamish. Blood and mucus rank low on my list of favorite bodily fluids. I'm pleased they exist, but I prefer knowing they're sealed within their intended containers. All through our labor and delivery classes I longed for the era when a man's presence in the delivery room not only wasn't required, it wasn't allowed.

I also photographed the birth, another unexpected course of action (I've never been a fan of the delivery room slide show foisted upon me by new parents). We have photos of our daughter emerging, and of the physicians holding her triumphantly in the air. We have photographs of her first wondering glimpse of her mother, and of her staring intently into the camera's lens when she was eight hours old. The photographs are precious, but redundant. The calm wisdom in that infant's eyes is something I will never forget.

Sofia emerged looking just like her father, which is unfortunate. I'm generally accepting of my image, but there's no doubt that my wife makes the better-looking woman. I hope that as Sofia grows she will resemble her mother more.

Driving myself home from the hospital before Elisa and Sofia's discharge, I had a spell of euphoria unequaled in my life. I was alone in the car, but I was giddy with pride. I thought to myself, I must be among the luckiest men to have ever lived. I have a wife I love boundlessly. I have a healthy baby daughter. I have a home and belongings far beyond the level of necessity, or even comfort. To say I want for nothing is inaccurate. I have an overabundance of everything. The miracle of my own life was suddenly dwarfed by a new fact: I'd participated in the creation of a new one. I couldn't be happier to have been surpassed.

When I was a kid, one family joke was that I'd been adopted. It's not a very funny joke; in fact, in some contexts it could be considered a form of abuse. Still, I'm the one who cultivated the theory and extended its life. I bore little resemblance to my brother, sister, or parents when I was very young, either facially or in body type. Now I probably bear a stronger resemblance to both of my parents than either of my siblings. I have my mother's looks, and every syllable I utter, every exhalation, echoes my father's bearing. Now I have a daughter of my own, a refracted reflection of me.

There were many years when I wondered, with good reason, whether my parents would get to see me live past the very beginnings of adulthood. There were years when I wondered whether they'd see me married. Now they've seen both, and they've seen me with a child of my own. The only thing left to wonder is what my parents must have wondered during those same years: how much of my child's life I'll get to see.

Since the moment of my daughter's conception my perspective about everything has changed yet again. Just as I've reached a point where I've felt able to release the past, as opposed to trying to outrun it, every thought has turned in a new direction. Not toward what's approaching from behind. Not even toward what's happening right now. I'm looking to the future.

I've found myself energized in a way I can't recall from any period of my life. Instead of my usual tendency to procrastinate, I've been seizing the tasks at hand and ripping through them. I bulldozed us through our move to a new apartment, packing nearly every one of our one hundred and eighty boxes myself. I hauled those boxes up and down flights of stairs like a teenager. When paint needed to be applied, or furniture bought, or preparations made, I got the jobs done. I'm eating better foods and exercising. I've bought life insurance. It's not just myself I'm responsible for anymore. It's not just Elisa and me. There's a little baby who needs protection. The life insurance policy cost a bit more than the average man might pay, but not as much as I'd feared. After all the difficulty I've had trusting in the safety of my existence, buying that policy has calmed me down more than anything else. If an insurance company is willing to bet its money on me, I figure I must be safe.

In considering all the ways I'll need to plan for Sofia's well-being, I realize it's not a new passion that's gripped me and set me in motion. It's the same instinct that appeared twenty years ago, when mine was the life in need of protection. I intend to remain as ferocious in safe-guarding this new one as I was of my own. More so.

. . .

MY STRONGEST SENSATION, the first night Elisa and I sat staring into the penetrating eyes of our newborn daughter, was that my previous life—the one that had haunted me for so long, but that I'd finally made peace with—was about to be replaced by a far more interesting one.

"It's a new beginning," I said to Elisa.

After all, I'm forty-six years old. I've finally reached an age where it could be considered appropriate for me to be thinking about the yoke of mortality tightening around my neck. Instead, I feel like I'm starting over. Again.

"It's got me bristling with excitement," I told her. "I'm bursting with joy."

After all I've been through, it feels like I've just begun.

Acknowledgments

The most common question I'm asked when I mention the fact that I've written a book is, "How long did it take?"

There's no simple answer to this, as the books I've written haven't consistently been done in workaday fashion. Many of the stories contained within my books have been written, honed, read aloud in various venues, honed yet again, and then set aside while other stories were worked on or other projects engaged in. Then, trying to fit the stories together—either into a collection or into a traditional narrative—requires further adjustments to each, as well as the addition of more material still. Once a publisher is in place and deadlines set, then the more consistent daily work begins. Which is all to say that this book has been several years in the making—meaning I've imposed myself on a large number of people along the way.

As with my first book, I owe a great debt of gratitude to the people at the Naked Angels theater company, both in New York and Los Angeles. They've been tremendously supportive of me as a writer, and have always allowed me great privileges when I felt I needed a roomful of ears to test material on. In particular I'd like to thank Liz Benjamin, Joe Danisi, Stephanie Cannon, Jen DiMartino, Kim Mercado, Shark, and Kathleen Dennehy for the work they've done on the Tuesday Nights at 9 series.

In a similar vein, Beth Lapides, Greg Miller, and everyone associated with Say the Word in Los Angeles have generously offered me fantastic encouragement and a forum to make use of and enjoy.

Once a publishing house comes into the picture, some of life's sweetest ironies are put into play. The same people who like your material enough to put their reputations behind it become both your coaches and your critics. The level of grace I've been able to maintain under those onslaughts is probably one of my poorest records as a human being. For their wise guidance and consistent help (not to mention their patience with my occasional outbursts) I'm deeply indebted to two editors at Riverhead Books, Geoffrey Kloske and Jake Morrissey. They continued to have faith and contribute when it would have been easy to turn away. Also lending tremendous support there (and also enduring my relentless inquiries and opinionating) were Lisa Amoroso, Michael Barson, Sarah Bowlin, and any number of others I may have been merely introduced to, or never met at all, but who form a vast team that has offered me unflagging support. Eventually, a book becomes a product, and I'm proud of the product they've made out of mine.

I have been lucky to land within the sphere of influence of David Black, a literary agent of distinction, a man of wisdom and honor, and a calming force on some of my most frantic days. He's surrounded himself with a roster of equally fine coagents in Joy Tutella and Susan Raihoffer, all ably assisted by Gary Morris and David Larabell.

Perhaps the most put-upon of all are the friends, coworkers, cohorts, and acquaintances who read, listened, read again, and listened more until they couldn't put up with it any longer—all without a penny's compensation. I'm going to list them in no particular order, though one deserves special distinction. This book would not be in published form if it weren't for the generosity and friendship of Stephen Glass. He is a good friend, a terrific writer, and a good man.

Also aiding and abetting, in one way or another (and with some undoubtedly left out and angry): Lisa Kogan, friend, and editor extraordinaire; Jackie Reingold; Julie Hilden; Gus Rogerson; Paul McCrane; David Eigenberg; Barry Singer; Peter Mehlman; Dan Baron; Daniel Reitz; Lenore Zerman; Kay Liberman; Geoff Ashley; Jerome Butler; Robert Zimmerman; V. Morrison; Amy Tan; Neil Simon; Meg Wolitzer; Meghan Daum; Lance Armstrong; Lewis Black; Shae Kennedy; Liz Tuccillo; Tony Kushner; David Duchovny; Sarah Jessica Parker; P. Roth; Lisa Kussell; Stella Connell; Adam Somers and PEN USA; Enid Handler; Murry Handler; Robert Rosenheck; Cindy Capobianco; Lowell Handler; Jane Smith; Lillian Handler; Jules Feiffer; Jenny Allen; Tom Kapinos; Lou Fusaro; Matthew Blank, Bob Greenblatt, Peter Kellner, Faye Katz, and Showtime Networks; and of course, the incomparable Elisa Atti (man, oh, man she's good at a lot of things).